Nicole,
Wishing you
rest on your jour[ney]
Trust yourself & you got
this! ♡ Matt Turk

What They Don't Teach You in College

Discovering and Loving Yourself in Times of Transition

MEREDITH TRANK

WHAT THEY DON'T TEACH YOU IN COLLEGE
DISCOVERING AND LOVING YOURSELF IN TIMES OF TRANSITION

iUniverse books may be ordered through booksellers or by contacting:

iUniverse
1663 Liberty Drive
Bloomington, IN 47403
www.iuniverse.com
844-349-9409

Because of the dynamic nature of the Internet, any web addresses or links contained in this book may have changed since publication and may no longer be valid. The views expressed in this work are solely those of the author and do not necessarily reflect the views of the publisher, and the publisher hereby disclaims any responsibility for them.

Any people depicted in stock imagery provided by Getty Images are models, and such images are being used for illustrative purposes only. Certain stock imagery © Getty Images.

ISBN: 978-1-6632-3600-5 (sc)
ISBN: 978-1-6632-3599-2 (e)

Library of Congress Control Number: 2022903170

Print information available on the last page.

iUniverse rev. date: 03/25/2022

For anyone navigating the unknown

Contents

Introduction

As I type these words, I am 26 years old and four years out of college. These past four years have been tumultuous and confusing and lonely. I've changed jobs and cities and relationships more than I ever thought I would. I've felt lost and then found. I've felt like I've known exactly what I want to do with my life, only to have an identity crisis the next day. I've felt like I have failed so many times. And I've felt so alone in what I was experiencing nearly every time. Like no one could really understand what I was going through, or, if they did, they never mentioned it. Can I get an AMEN??

Many people tell you that college will be the best four years of your life. And yes, college is usually an assumably fun season of our lives where we have little responsibility and a lot of freedom. But college can also be hard. It can be a time of frustration, discomfort, and loneliness for some. When the emphasis is only on your college experience, you kind of forget that there is life after college that you may or may not be prepared for. No one ever warns you about the abyss of the unknown you are about to step into. And I'm not just talking about all the things you need to know for "adulting," like how to do your taxes or transition off your parent's health insurance. I'm talking about the emotional rollercoaster of an identity crisis nearly every 20-something goes through when they graduate college, pursue a career, start a relationship, you name it. I think every senior graduating college needs to enroll in a class their final semester called "Life After College: What To Do When You Realize You Don't Know What To Do." That would have been super helpful.

But alas, most of us did not get such a course on life, so we got sent out into the world under the illusion that we would be unstoppable with our degrees in hand. We would obviously get a job in said degree's field and then make enough money to be comfortable and still have the same best friends from college and automatically discover an adult-version of college community. Life would go on without a hitch. Well, if you're reading this and you're out of college, then you don't need me to tell you that that is not how this story goes. It is unfortunate but true, and I'm sick of people sugar coating life after college. It's tough, confusing, and often disappointing. I'm not trying to be a Debbie-downer, just being real here.

The seasons of unknown in our lives can be super discouraging. We tend to feel alone, stuck, and down on ourselves because something has changed in our lives that we did not want to change. You didn't want that relationship to end or to graduate college or to move to that city you discover you actually hate. We start to realize that we aren't in control of everything, which is a brutal wake-up call. There is pressure to make all the "right" decisions, but no one tells you what those are. It's almost as though you had permission to discover yourself in college, but once you graduate, you're supposed to have that figured out. But the truth is that the journey to discovering ourselves takes our entire life.

A significant part of my continual self-discovery journey included figuring out what I believe about God. I grew up in the Episcopal church then switched over to a non-denominational community, only to feel even more challenged and confused by what I believed and what I was experiencing. Today, I don't claim a certain Christian denomination, and it's taken me a while to be at peace with that. Spiritual belonging isn't always found in organized religion, and I believe that God is bigger than the institutions we try and put God in. I've always been fascinated by God and religion, so much so that I studied it in undergrad and have now completed a Master of Divinity degree. Really all this means is that I am curious about how people understand the divine and how our spirituality impacts our lives. So we are going to talk about what that relationship with the divine looks like for you and how your belief about God or the Universe influences your beliefs about yourself. Whether we like it or not, these beliefs are intertwined, and they do influence one another. Our journeys of self-discovery will require open-mindedness to expand our beliefs about ourselves and about God. If what we explore together challenges you, that is a good thing. Growth does not happen in our comfort zones, and God is big enough to handle our questions and confusions.

I believe God speaks to us through our experiences, but the problem is, most of us don't take the time to listen. We rush through life, blaming our external circumstances for the hard stuff while crediting ourselves with the good stuff. God isn't picky, though, and will use both the good and the bad to speak to us. And when we take time to reflect on those experiences and even share those learnings with others, we see that we are way less alone in what we go through than we think. We are much more alike than we are different. Our shared experiences are more common than we realize. We all face similar struggles and go through similar seasons in life. Even the uncertain ones.

During my unknown seasons, I wanted to read words from someone in the thick of what I was experiencing. It was still comforting and assuring to read words from people in older years of life looking back on this time and sharing what they've learned, but I needed a confused-as-hell 28-year-old to tell me that I'm okay. I wanted to read words that said, "Meredith, you are NOT alone in how confused you feel. You don't need to keep looking outside yourself for the answers. You can trust what you know and who you are from within. You got this." It was exhausting looking to others to determine how I should feel and what I should do. And it took a long time and a lot of heartbreak to get to a place where I finally trusted myself.

I'm not saying I want to "save" you from these hard experiences because I believe they are probably what brought you here to this book. Something happened, something changed in your life, and now you're here, in the unknown, maybe a little stuck, unsure of what to do next. I mean, I rarely know what to eat for lunch, let alone what my next step in life should be. Friend, you are not alone in the depth of the confusion you feel right now. I am with you.

Think of this book as a navigation guide or as your best friend sitting on your couch for wine night. This is your voice of self-compassion. This is your permission to be uncertain and confused. This is a trusted friend telling you that it's actually okay to be stuck.

Here, in the unknown, there is no way out but through, and we all go at a different pace. But I believe this time of uncertainty can and will lead you to your truest self as we discover who you are and what you want.

If you are feeling stuck in a transition, unsure of what next step to take, this book is for you. If you feel lost and confused about who you are and what you want, this book is for you. If you are sick of giving others power over how you should be living your life, this book is for you. If you are struggling to embrace the radiant human God made you to be, this book is for you. I believe our journey of self-discovery is beautiful and worthwhile, and now, during an unknown season, is the best time to take that dive into knowing yourself.

We're going to start by defining what the heck this transitional, liminal, unknown season of life might look like for you and what this means for your growth. Then we will look at your beliefs about God, yourself, and your potential, for you will soon learn how foundational those three beliefs are to your self-discovery journey. We will throw the "shoulds" of other people out the window and learn how to start digging deeper within to live in alignment with our wants, values, and needs. We will explore the meaning of vocation, that thing you do in life (and no I'm not just talking about your "job" here), and how to make decisions that take you one step closer to it. And finally, we will talk through confidence and impostor syndrome and how you can own who you truly are. No more looking outside yourself for a sense of worth or solidarity. You will get to a place where you confidently know who you are, and you will believe that person is worthy of what you want.

Throughout the book, you will see me reference and quote a lot of other folks who have done insightful work to help us navigate this season of life. Like I said, while I really needed the voice of another confused twenty-something to help me through the unknown, I also recognized that I needed the perspective of those who have more experience and expertise than I do. So, since I don't want to pretend to be anything I am not and my experience is limited to my own, I am leaning on the gift of wisdom from many other experts to help us navigate this unknown time. You will hear from theologians, psychologists, authors, and fellow-human-beings whose knowledge will help us better understand what we are going through and how we can move through it. By leaning on experts who have done years of education and research, we can more confidently trust that we are being guided by legitimate voices, concepts, theories, and experiences.

At the end of each chapter, I will offer a few reflection questions and prompts to help you process and think through the content. Becoming more self-aware is a significant component of our self-discovery journeys, so do not feel like you need to rush through this book like it's a box you need to check. Again, we are all growing at our own pace. I encourage you to have a journal with you as you read this book so you can reflect on what you might be discovering about yourself and how it is impacting you. It can also be helpful to refer back to in the future for when you feel lost or stuck again. If you simply read the book without doing the work, I cannot guarantee that you will see much progress. I know it might be uncomfortable at times, but we do not grow in our comfort zones. Take the time to think through and write down your answers to the reflection questions, especially when you feel resistance to do so. That's when the work really happens.

When you live in alignment with the person God made you to be, I believe you become filled with freedom, joy, and peace. My goal in sharing these words is to help you feel less alone in your unknown season, discover your most authentic needs, values, and desires, and then give the practical encouragement you need to fiercely go after them. **I want you to not only know who you truly are, but love who you are and believe that person is worth celebrating and fighting for each day.** No matter what circumstances we find ourselves in, I believe we have the power to honor our truest selves each day, thus leaving us feeling whole and loved.

There's no pressure here. No pressure to perform or do this work perfectly. Because news flash: you can't. There is no one-right-way to self-discovery, but I do believe this time of uncertainty is a great starting point. **When we feel the most lost is when we desire to be**

the most found. Take advantage of this gift of the unknown and be patient with yourself. The journey to discovering all of us might take a lifetime, but it's a journey worth taking. It will take some trial and error, but I hope the practices I can share here will help you know how to return to yourself every time. I want you to leave this book, and maybe also this difficult season of life, with concrete, real tools that you can use moving forward when you enter these unknown seasons again.

Know that I am immensely grateful you chose to read this book. This book is a product of my own self-discovery journey during the time of Covid-19, and I put a lot of pressure on myself for it to be perfect. But perfect is never the goal, only progress. Only learning. Only love. My hope is that you'll learn to love the truest version of yourself throughout these pages and believe that person is worth fighting for. Let's do this.

1

THE IN-BETWEEN

I DID NOT WANT TO graduate from college. I know most students look forward to graduating from college more than anything, but for the few weirdos like me who love school, I was totally in denial that it was ending. On graduation day, I could barely pry myself out of bed to go to the commencement ceremony. A day that was supposed to be filled with celebration and excitement was one of dismay for me. Why? It was quite simple. I didn't want college to end because I didn't want to lose my identity.

At that point in my life, all my identities were wrapped up in things related to being in college. I was defined by the organizations I was involved in, my friend groups, my relationships, my jobs, my grades, my sorority, all of it. I had been a student for the past 19 years of my life, so WHAT was I going to be now? And the change happened as fast as the switch of a light. The day after graduation, I already had friends moving to new states, starting new jobs, and moving on to new identities. And while I was blessed to have a job starting at the beginning of June, I had a few weeks to wait it out and navigate this new, uncertain time.

Those few weeks between graduation and training for my new job were rough, to say the least. I was turning to everything outside of myself to feel better and cope with the loss and confusion of being between two seasons of life. I was grieving the loss of my friends being near me with alcohol and partying. I tried to "make the most" of my time in my college town by keeping my schedule as busy as possible. I think I had a coffee date literally every day because I was so afraid I would lose touch with anyone I knew there. I felt utterly and totally lost.

One morning, after a few weeks of wild Meredith roaming the streets, I remember returning to the house my two best friends and

1

I lived in throughout college. They had already moved out, so I was packing up to move into my temporary living space for the summer. I got dropped off at the house, slightly hungover, and went to our bathroom, which had the most disgusting pink tile. I placed both my hands on the edges of the sink, took a deep breath, and tears began to well in my eyes. I looked in the mirror and began to weep as I didn't even recognize the woman looking back at me.

Who had I become? Why had I made so many bad choices regarding coping with graduation and all these changes? Where were my roommates? Where was my LIFE? How had everything changed so quickly?

There, in that empty house, staring at my unhappy, unrecognizable reflection in the mirror, I finally accepted where I was at in life. Completely lost. Completely in-between.

Liminality

I hate going to the doctor. Not so much because of the doctors themselves, but because of the waiting room experience. My anxiety is magnified by just sitting in the waiting room for my appointment. As a kid, my mom always made us show up thirty minutes early to any appointment, which I dreaded because I knew that would extend my time in the intolerable waiting room. Whenever they called my name, and I was with the doctor, it was fine, but all the waiting really stressed me out.

And what is it about waiting rooms anyway? Are they all required to stock their tables with the same magazines like *O* and *Southern Living*? Very not-young-person friendly options, if you ask me. And the smell of the waiting room. I know you know what I am talking about here. It is the most distinct, stale smell on planet earth that just triggers my senses into being stressed.

The worst appointments for me, the ones that cause the most turmoil, are the yearly check-ups. There is nothing wrong with me. There is no reason I need to go to the doctor other than to check in and make sure everything is okay, but my fear lies in the worry that this will be the appointment where they find "the thing." You know, that thing that's wrong with you? I'm going to sit down, put my little gown on, and they are going to start examining me only to find something irreversibly wrong. Has this ever happened to me? No. Do I catastrophize every single doctor's appointment I go to? Yes.

This, my friends, is a clear example of wanting to be in control mixed with giving my anxiety power over my experience. When I'm in the waiting room, I am living in fear of the unknown future. I am unwilling to surrender control of my circumstances. I am so afraid of the "what ifs" of a doctor's appointment that I rob myself of being present with where I am right then and there. Worrying about some uncertain, unlikely future outcome will not do me any good in the present moment. Frankly, it is only going to make things worse. So I might as well take a deep breath, settle in, and crack open that 2016 *O* magazine sitting next to me.

The waiting room at the doctor is a lot like liminality. You are anxiously occupying the threshold of learning something new about yourself. The waiting room is uncomfortable, maybe a little itchy and smelly. It seems like time goes on forever. You sit a little taller and perk up every time a nurse comes out the door asking to see the next patient, only for you to be let down when it isn't you. You are ready for the next opportunity to come just so you can leave the dang waiting room. Sometimes you don't even care what awaits you on the other side! You just want to be out of the unknown.

The metaphorical waiting rooms in our lives can cause a lot of disruption in our souls. It is hard to be stuck in-between one thing and the next, not knowing when the time will come for you to be called to move on. This in-between space is also referred to as liminal space, or as one of my professors would call it, "being betwixt and between." Julia Thomas with Better Help Counseling defines liminal space as, "transitional or transformative spaces. They are the waiting areas between one point in time and space and the next."[1] Big life transformations can take place in liminal spaces. Being in-between means you are on the brink of something new in your life. You are on the cusp of discovering a more authentic self, if you allow yourself to be open to it. Author and priest Richard Rohr describes liminal space this way, "The threshold is God's waiting room. Here we are taught openness and patience as we come to expect appointment with the divine Doctor."[2] Openness and patience. Ah yes, we could all be seeking a bit more of that. Staying open-minded is the key to transformation in this liminal time. If you keep an open mind, you never know how God can move.

Liminal space is defined as a threshold, where you are on the cusp of one thing ending and a new thing beginning. Or, as I like to think of it, you're in the Britney Spears' song *I'm Not A Girl, Not Yet A Woman.* In their book *The Discerning Heart,* Wilkie and Noreen Cannon Au describe the three stages of not-knowing as separation, liminality, and reincorporation. They write:

> In the first phase, initiants are ritually separated from the social group that until then defined their cultural roles and identities and removed to a secluded place… Removal from society inaugurates the second phase of initiation, the liminal phase. **The goal of the liminal phase is to bring about a personal transformation that enables people to redefine who they are and to reorient their lives in terms of this new identity and consciousness.** When the liminal phase is completed, reincorporation rites signal their reentry into the social group as a "new" person.[3]

Au and Au write about liminality in terms of rituals because, more often than not, certain rites are included when moving from one stage of life to another. Again, in my example, the tradition was the graduation ceremony, signifying I was losing my identity as a student and moving into the adult world. Some of you might be in a clearly defined liminal season of life, but some of you may not be. Maybe you were furloughed or laid off, which you were not expecting at all. There was no ceremony or ritual to initiate your time into liminality, yet here you are. It is still legitimate and still real whether you had a formal tradition ushering you into the unknown or it just happened to you.

Now you are separated from something. You are no longer with that company or at that church or in that school. Something is lost. And when we lose valuable things, it is healthy and essential that we grieve. We must take the time we need to be sad and cry and cope with the loss. This liminal space is the ideal opportunity you have to transform. You are moving from one identity to the next, but here, in the middle, is where you decide what this new identity is. You have the chance to redefine who you are and what you want in the world without the unwelcome influence of others.

Often we go to the doctor because we are sick, and sometimes, they can provide a quick solution. Other times, the doctor might prescribe a medicine where it could take weeks for us to feel better while it is fighting off whatever has infected us. Or, in the case of a virus, there is no quick solution, and we just have to wait for the pain to go away. We are not the doctors in this situation, only the patients, and we can trust that the doctor knows what they are doing. They are the expert here, and we trust our healing into their care, no matter how long it might take to see results. As Rohr says, God is our divine doctor, and God can and will provide the healing you seek. The healing might not come on our perfect timeline, but it will come.

In this liminal season, unwelcome reminders of hurtful pasts might arise. You might discover you need healing in a particular area you didn't know you did. Or something might remind you of that painful happening that you've tried to forget. Overall, as you are experiencing a loss, there might be resentment or anger that needs healing. It is good, beautiful, and essential to recognize that you need help, and you never need to feel ashamed to ask for it.

Similar to the experience at the doctor, healing from our divine doctor can have different timelines. Sometimes it can feel like a quick fix, and other times, the healing process can take forever. I know it sucks to have to wait and be patient for healing to come. I know it doesn't always look like we want it to. And I know sometimes, more often than not, honestly, the healing takes way longer than we want it to. We can feel like we are in the waiting room forever, waiting for God to step in and provide healing and a next step. Together we are going to stop anxiously looking at the door and instead breathe, ground ourselves in trust, and read our *Southern Living* as we wait.

If and when fears and past hurts arise in the waiting, know that is normal and welcome. You are not broken if you experience moments or seasons of pain and anxiety in the unknown. Don't suppress what arises. We will learn how to work through the healing. We will learn how to trust God as our healer when we don't want to. We will learn to see waiting as a gift to be received as it leads us to greater discovery of ourselves for when we move on to our next steps.

Like Rohr says, I believe openness and patience will allow the sacred to move in this secular, waiting season of your life. Instant gratification is not always of the divine, so stay wary of quick fixes or easy, temporary solutions. **Don't be afraid to let the sacred in, for I believe God has a lot to show you in this waiting period if you let God move.** As theologian and mystic Howard Thurman said, this is a time in your life where you can find your genuine self. He writes, "There is something in every one of you that waits and listens for the sound of the genuine in yourself. It is the only true guide you will ever have. And if you cannot hear it, you will all of your life spend your days on the ends of strings that somebody else pulls."[4] No longer will you live a life someone else has chosen for you. You have the gift of time and space to finally quiet down the outside noise and listen to the sound of your genuine. And once we have heard it, we must honor it.

Don't Run

Rohr also describes liminal space as the time "when you have left, or are about to leave, the tried and true, but have not yet been able to replace it with anything else. It is when you are between your old comfort zone and any possible new answer. If you are not trained in how to hold anxiety, how to live with ambiguity, how to entrust and wait, you will run...anything to flee this terrible cloud of unknowing."[5] And run I did during that month between graduating college and starting my first job. I ran to alcohol, to men, to parties, to social media, to food, really to anything that would distract and fill my uncomfortable void of unknowing. I was lost. I had no idea who I was anymore, so I filled and did whatever I could to make myself feel loved and happy and seen.

But sometimes, we just need to sit in the discomfort of the unknown times. And, as Rohr says, my hope in this book is that you, unlike me, will be trained in holding anxiety and living well in this in-between. I hope you can thrive in this unknown space and discover the keys to your freedom moving forward. I want you to know from the beginning that you are not alone, and you are loved. All of us will experience the in-between at some point in time, and it is my hope that this resource can help you walk through it.

When we are going through a time of transition, it usually begins with the loss of something. Something is taken from you, something is lost, or something changes. In this particular example I just shared, my loss was that college ended. This change could also look like losing or quitting a job. It could be ending a relationship or being broken up with. Ultimately, it doesn't matter if the change is initiated by you or not. It just matters that it has happened. Even when it is a change that we think we want because we control it, it still brings a season of transition and unknown. And that can still come with grief.

With any kind of loss of identity, we have two choices. We can stay the same, or we can change. We can see this space of unknown time as a punishment for the change in our lives, or we can see it as an opportunity to become more self-aware and integrated. We can use the unknown time we've been given as a gift.

This is time for you to see where your identity was possibly too heavily placed in something out there and not enough in here. There must be a healthy balance between both your external and internal identity. Some of our external identities, like our jobs, give us meaning in life that is valuable to hold onto. Still, it must be balanced with an internal sense of worth. I want you to be confident in who you are from the inside out, not depending on the outside version of you to define who you are.

This loss or change does not only have to look like a job change or a move to a new city. It doesn't only mean external things, but it can also be internal. Maybe you are wrestling with your gender identity or sexuality. Or maybe your beliefs are changing and how you once thought ideologically, politically, or religiously are no longer in alignment with who you are. You are now in a discovery phase of these new beliefs you hold. However you are experiencing transition, know that this book is here to help you feel confident and knowledgeable in who you are, what you believe, and what you want.

I want to help you own and find your identity and peace in the midst of the unknown. I want you to be confident based on what is true and beautiful about you when you don't have direction and are scared to try something new. I want you to believe you can step into the new season of life with the assurance that you are enough. And that no matter how things change, there are some unshakeable truths about your humanity that can hold you in uncertain times.

In this book, I'm going to push you, and I will ask you to be honest with yourself. We won't grow if we choose to run from ourselves and our real feelings. We have to sit in the discomfort to move forward. We have to grieve our losses and then pivot toward a new perspective. You can get through this, and you WILL get through this. It is my hope that we will see you on the other side of this in-between, more confident in the beautiful person you are than when we began.

So, are you ready to dig in? Are you ready to make the most of this liminal space? Are you ready to learn what they didn't teach you in college?

Start Here:

1. How do you feel in this moment, as we start this journey together?
2. What worries or fears might you have as you dive into this work?
3. What identity do you feel you have lost in this time?
4. What do you hope to gain by the end of this book?
5. Who do you want to be on the other side of the unknown?

2

Unshakeable Truths

ON MY FIRST DAY OF Divinity School, the Dean of Admission came into our classroom to discuss the "rules" of academic life. She went over things you might expect like the code of conduct, consequences for plagiarism, and other basic expectations. Toward the end, she introduced a new topic that I had never encountered before, though. She began to talk about our language for God and how it needed to be inclusive. This was something I had never even thought about. I figured everyone thought of God as their Father who was in Heaven! She shared that some people have a hurtful or harmful image of God. They might feel more comfortable naming God as Universe, Spirit, Higher Power, Creator, or whatever resonates best with them instead of God. She also encouraged us to use gender-neutral language when talking about God. In all the Bibles I owned and had read throughout my life, God was He, so I literally had never questioned this before. I had to become very mindful of this right away and began replacing my "he" in all my work with "God." Instead of himself, it's Godself, and instead of He watches over us, it's God watches over us. Although there can be a lot of "God" in a sentence sometimes, it's important when I consider the impact solely masculine language could have in preventing someone from connecting with God.

The Divinity School I attended celebrates diversity and encourages different points of view and perspectives. I am so grateful I did my master's work in this program because before this, I only had one way of understanding God and the Bible...my own. Now, my views have been challenged and expanded for the better and are more inclusive. I mean, who decided that God was a "he" in the first place? Men, that's who! And how does anyone actually know who

God is? Does God even have a gender? Does God need to have a gender for us to be able to relate to God? Welcome to my theological-question-filled brain.

I had a belief about God that I thought to be true because it had never been challenged or questioned. I always assumed God was our Father, but I had never stopped to consider what that really meant or could imply. Did I really believe God was a dad up in the heavenly skies? What about those who had an abusive dad or could never know their father? What does God as Father mean to them? It's probably relatively harmful and problematic, so that is something that needs to be considered. I was totally on board with being more inclusive, but I would never have even seen this blind spot in my theology if it weren't for someone helping me challenge it.

It is essential you take time to recognize and consider the foundational beliefs you have held true for your life as you begin your self-discovery journey. There might be some unshakeable truths you currently hold about yourself and God that have never been challenged or reconsidered. And there are specific prerequisites you must believe are true for you so you can move forward on this journey with full freedom to discover your most authentic self. I want you to have the expansive opportunity to imagine God however you need to and own whatever parts of you that you are afraid to let shine. I want to encourage you to view God, and yourself, in a new way so you can go deeper in your journey.

What you believe about God and what you believe about yourself will define how you navigate this season. If your view of yourself is limited, set with stark views of right and wrong, then you will not get very far because you will prevent yourself from reaching your full potential. And if you believe God is up in the sky as some puppet master directing your life and you get no say, then there is not much agency you will find in the choices you can make in the here and now. So we are going to dive into these two ideas a little further. Let's begin with exploring your God belief.

God Belief

Depending on your religious upbringing, your current beliefs, and your stage of life, everyone reading this book will approach their belief in God differently. Let me be the first to own how much my beliefs about God change. I've already shared how some of them have changed because someone simply encouraged me to widen my understanding of the divine. It's natural and good to let some beliefs change and to question them as we grow. We are evolving individuals, so it would only make sense that our spiritual lives would evolve, as well.

I believe that for us to move through this liminal time with hope on the other side, we have to develop a healthy, trusting belief in God. We have to believe that the Universe has our back. That up there, the Higher Power wants you to be free. It wants you to discover these true things about yourself. **God wants you to live in full freedom of who you were created to be.**

Just think about it! If you genuinely believe that God wants what is best for you, you will more willingly surrender this season to your Creator. But, if you don't trust God and if you do not believe God cares for your utmost wellbeing, then you will close your fist and take back all the power and stress as you move through this transition. The Message version of Matthew 7:7-11 reads,

> Don't bargain with God. Be direct. Ask for what you need. This isn't a cat-and-mouse, hide-and-seek game we're in. If your child asks for bread, do you trick him with sawdust? If he asks for fish, do you scare him with a live snake on his plate? As bad as you are, you wouldn't think of such a thing. You're at least decent to your own children. So don't you think the God who conceived you in love will be even better?

Essentially, what Jesus is saying here is to consider the people you love in your life the most, whether that be a child, a partner, or a friend. Now, suppose that person came to you earnestly asking for something they need. In that case, even if you couldn't provide exactly what they wanted, you will do your very best to provide for them at that moment. Why? Because you love them! You care about them, and when they are direct in asking for what they need, you will do your best to provide. Unless you are a really shitty friend, you aren't going to deceive the one you love when they really need you.

God is our Divine Parent. **God created you and me with every intention of seeing us flourish as free beings in this world.** God sees the big picture and the minute details. God wants you to live into the gifts God gave you. And since God is the One who loves us more than we could ever love another human on earth, it makes logical sense that when we earnestly ask God for what we need, God will deliver. This doesn't mean instant gratification, and this doesn't mean God will give us everything we want, but God answers. God provides. God guides. God is our Waymaker, and we are co-creators with God in this life we live.

Skirt! Rewind. Did you just say I was a co-creator with God? Somehow, I have the same power that God does? No, no, that's not what I was taught. That can't be true. Well, remember, we are here to welcome a little challenge to the current beliefs we might hold. If you just got uncomfortable reading that, then GOOD! We are in the right starting place. God is not so small that our Creator can't handle a little discomfort and new ways of thinking. God casts a net wide enough to encompass all our understandings and curiosities about the divine.

Consider this. God is both transcendent and immanent. God is omnipotent and big and over all the world. And God is also so close that God sees and understands and cares for all your minor concerns. In her book, *The Way of Discernment,* Elizabeth Liebert writes, "God leaves us quite free to determine the specifics of our lives, while at the same time providing us with a climate of love, care, salvation, and grace in which to grow to maturity."[6] God is not a puppet-master running the world and controlling all your decisions while you get zero say in the matter. That's called a lack of free will, and that's not how God operates.

You get a choice here. You get to co-create your life with God. And while that might be frustrating because you want to predict the future when you're going through challenging, unknown times like this, I hope this excites you to know you have control here. And, as Liebert writes, God is with you as you navigate this liminal season every step of the way.

I like to envision God sometimes as a heated blanket. Specifically, a cheetah print heated blanket so I can feel fabulous as I'm feeling warm. When I think of God, I think of being wrapped in my heated, fierce blanket of love. Being in that blanket makes me feel safe, warm, cared for, and like no matter what, I'm okay in this moment. As many wise people have said before me, when I am wrapped up in my heated blanket of God's grace, I truly hear the Spirit say *all shall be well.* That's God y'all. God is wrapping you in a heated blanket of love as you move through this season and make decisions going forward. And God cares about what you want and who you want to be. You have some agency here, so don't be afraid to own it.

What you believe about God will directly affect the freedom you feel in this season. It will shape your daily attitudes and perspectives. If you don't think you get a say in the direction of your life and it's just going to happen to you, then you won't try. If you don't think God wants the best for you, then you won't trust. But if you believe God loves you and wants you to live into your authentic self, then you'll grow as you discover another layer of who God made you to be.

What if you truly believed that owning and living in alignment with every piece of you, your deepest desires, your scariest questions, your unspoken dreams, all of it, was actually all that God wants for you? What if fully loving God meant fully loving yourself? What if honoring God looked like honoring your deepest needs, values, and dreams? **What if discovering more of God meant discovering more of you?**

If you can lean in and even just begin to believe or desire some of those things to ring true for you, then you are on the right path. You don't have to fully commit and say yes to them all in this moment. Remember, we are evolving. There is no rush or time limit to this process. I mean, this is honestly a journey we will be on for our whole lives, and I believe it's one worth taking. If you haven't taken the first step, now is the best time to do so. The unknown is the ideal time for exploration.

Self-Belonging

As we navigate liminal spaces, it will be tempting to look everywhere except within ourselves for the answers to what we should do or who we should be. To combat this temptation, we need a strong sense of self-belonging, which I define as a sense of self that is so secure it doesn't depend on outside factors to make it whole. No other person, job, or circumstance completes someone who has a strong sense of self-belonging. These people are genuinely content because they can rest confidently in who they are.

We are all wired for belonging. Self-belonging is when you get clear on your needs, values, and dreams and know you are living in alignment with them. It's a matter of integrity coupled with self-acceptance. It's accepting where you are at and not compromising on what is true for you. When you belong to yourself and know that you are making decisions that honor your authentic self, you will emerge confident no matter what life throws at you. Dr. Brené Brown defines True Belonging as,

> the **spiritual practice** of **believing in and belonging to yourself** so deeply that you can **share your most authentic self** with the world and **find sacredness** in being both **a part of something** and **standing alone** in the wilderness. True belonging doesn't require you to change who you are; it requires you to be who you are.[7]

Now, let's break this down a bit. True belonging starts as a spiritual practice. You might be wondering, what does finding my sense of belonging have to do with spirituality? Does this mean I need to be part of a church to find my belonging? Don't get too far away from me here. Give me a chance to explain.

I believe what Dr. Brown is saying is that the work of truly believing in and belonging to yourself requires practices and disciplines that transcend the physical. Cultivating self-belonging cannot be done or found simply by looking around you. Rather, you have to look within. You have to be willing to get still, find solitude, and get a little uncomfortable with yourself before finding confidence in owning who you are. Self-discovery thrives in the quiet. You might find yourself standing alone in the messiness in this liminal season of life. When you are in-between, it is hard to feel like you belong to yourself or a community. You're figuring things out, and that is totally okay and totally normal. It is the perfect opportunity to find belonging within yourself.

My hope for you is that you can, as Dr. Brown says, find sacredness in the discovery of yourself in this time. Liminal spaces are often where the sacred and the secular meet. It is that threshold, the meeting place of the divine and the every day. It can leave you vulnerable and open for God to transform you.

There are many reasons why you might find yourself in a liminal season of life right now. But what is sure is that something changed, and now you find yourself in an uncertain time. This often correlates with some sort of power being taken from you. It might look like change within your job, your circumstances, or your identity, but shifts in power are uncomfortable for us all. When you become familiar and comfortable with something, or, simply put, when you feel as though you are in control, you feel powerful, and that feels good. But, in this time of transition, that power has been taken away. You might, at this moment, feel as though you have no control over what has happened or what will happen in the future. That's totally normal. Our personal feeling of power is crucial to unpack at the start of your journey to self-discovery because you must believe you have power over this. Your choices matter. God wants what is best for you. You can do this.

Start Here:

1. What foundational beliefs about God might you need to reconsider?
2. How do you feel about believing you are a co-creator with God?
3. How is your current sense of self-belonging? Do you feel at peace and at home with yourself?
4. How might you begin to see this liminal time as a sacred opportunity?
5. Are you comfortable letting God move in this season? Do you trust that the Universe has your back? Take some time here to explore why or why not.

3

You've Got the Power

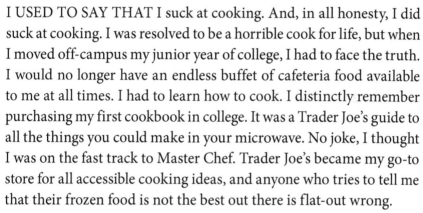

I USED TO SAY THAT I suck at cooking. And, in all honesty, I did suck at cooking. I was resolved to be a horrible cook for life, but when I moved off-campus my junior year of college, I had to face the truth. I would no longer have an endless buffet of cafeteria food available to me at all times. I had to learn how to cook. I distinctly remember purchasing my first cookbook in college. It was a Trader Joe's guide to all the things you could make in your microwave. No joke, I thought I was on the fast track to Master Chef. Trader Joe's became my go-to store for all accessible cooking ideas, and anyone who tries to tell me that their frozen food is not the best out there is flat-out wrong.

Once I graduated college and started adulting on my own, I figured I might need to start learning how to cook more. Expanding my pallet beyond Trader Joe's frozen orange chicken just felt like the right move. My husband, Michael, and I had just started dating, and he is a phenomenal cook. He loves trying out audacious recipes and dishes and is truly someone who can look at a lineup of spices and know just which ones to use in a dish. So, I started where any budding chef would begin, a HelloFresh subscription.

Before I knew it, I had conveniently delivered boxes with all the ingredients I needed for three meals a week to prepare and devour. And, they were delicious! And, I made them all by myself! And, nine times out of ten, I didn't royally mess them up! Sure, they may not all have been Instagram-worthy masterpieces. Still, they were nutritious, delicious meals I could be proud of preparing. Sometimes I would eat them all on my own, but the best was when I would cook and have Michael come over to eat with me. I felt so much joy and pride knowing that I worked hard to prepare something that nourished his body. I now understood why he, and so many others, love to cook.

It's probably less about how good it makes them feel and rather how good it feels when they get to serve others. I used to joke and say that cooking was more stress-inducing than stress-relieving for me. And while it honestly is still not my favorite go-to activity, I don't dread it, and I do enjoy it.

Throughout my cooking journey, I went from having a fixed mindset, I cannot cook, to a growth mindset, I want to learn how to cook. At first, I honestly thought and believed I was just a lousy cook. I felt discouraged by it and embarrassed by all the times I "failed" at it. I was unwilling to see my potential. I just sulked and complained and dealt with it because it was something that I didn't want to change about myself. But, because of Michael and honestly, because it is a pretty essential skill to have in life, I forced myself to adopt a growth mindset and develop my potential. It has taken time to get to where I am today regarding my confidence in the kitchen. Sometimes I still catch myself getting defensive when Michael tries to gently correct me regarding how I chop an onion. I am willing to accept the feedback most of the time, though, because I recognize I don't have to be perfect at this thing. I just have to be willing to learn.

When it comes to your personal self-discovery journey, you must have a growth mindset. If you don't believe you have the potential to change, then you won't! Remember our conversation about believing you have the power to co-create with God? Well, coupled with your God Belief is the belief you have in yourself to grow and change. This, my friends, is the growth mindset.

Growth Mindset

Psychologist Dr. Carol Dweck is most known for her work on defining both fixed and growth mindsets. She has conducted years of studies on people of all ages and demographics to discover how these mindsets affect the choices we make and the lives we live. These two mindsets are all about the difference in how we see our potential and will significantly impact how we approach this time. Do we believe we can grow and change and live into this new version of ourselves we discover? Or do we think that how we are now is fixed? How quickly do we allow "failure" to define us, or can we see setbacks as opportunities for growth?

If I could look you deep in the eyes and hold your shoulders in this moment as I type this to you, I would, but hear me bearing into your soul when I say you are not a failure. I don't care what has happened to bring you to this liminal, unknown season, but if for a second you are considering that it is because you are a failure, then that is a lie! **You are not a failure.** You are a beautiful human being that life happened to. Shit happens to everyone. There are endless things outside of our control. Don't beat yourself up for being in the unknown. Certainty does not equate to success, so don't think for a second think that just because you are in-between or because something changed that you have failed.

Our mindset and perspective must be rooted in a place of possibility and openness before we embark on our self-discovery journey. You might discover that you want to change and grow in specific ways. That is fantastic, but we must have a growth mindset if we're going to be empowered to actually make those changes. We can't stay stuck thinking that our potential is fixed and how we are today is how we will always be. If you believe that you are a co-creator with God, then you have some control over how your life goes. Let's seize it.

Dr. Dweck helps us understand these two mindsets. She says that the fixed mindset is the belief that your qualities are carved in stone, and this "creates an urgency to prove yourself over and over."[8] Rather, the growth mindset is "based on the belief that your basic qualities are things you can cultivate through your efforts, your strategies, and help from others."[9] Dr. Dweck boldly claims that the growth mindset is what allows people to thrive during the most challenging times of their lives. She emphasizes that this truly is a choice that we can make, so I encourage you to choose wisely and choose to grow in this time.

Show yourself grace if this mental switch doesn't happen immediately. For those of us in a fixed mindset, it can be really life-altering to suddenly change your belief about yourself. Moving from a mindset that facts are facts about ourselves to one where we can learn and grow can be really disorienting at first. That's the thing about the two mindsets. The fixed mindset thinks it has to be naturally "good" at something to do it, so if you can't do something, you just shouldn't try. But the growth mindset believes in your ability to cultivate your potential, and that in itself is fulfilling. Those with the growth mindset cope with setbacks using determination. On this, Dr. Dweck writes,

> Believing talents can be developed allows people to fulfill their potential…The growth mindset *does* allow people to love what they're doing – and to continue to love it in the face of difficulties…It's ironic: The top is where the fixed-mindset people hunger to be, but it's where the growth-minded people arrive as a by-product of their enthusiasm for what they do…In the fixed mindset, everything is about the outcome. If you fail – or if you're not the best – it's all been wasted. The growth mindset allows people to value what they're doing *regardless of the outcome.*[10]

This is an important lesson to consider on our self-discovery journey. Instead of focusing intently on the outcome, let's focus on the process. Maybe you are hoping for a new job on the other side of this liminal season. That's a great goal! What is just as crucial as getting the job, though, is who you become along the way. How you make the adjustments you need to live your life in alignment with who you truly are is what will ultimately lead you to "success." **Focus on your journey, and then you can more easily trust the outcome.**

Throughout this book and your self-discovery journey, we will identify your needs, values, and dreams to confidently go after what you want in life. Now, this might include some things you aren't "good" at yet, but that's okay. It's the **yet** that is important here. For this journey to work, you have to believe in your potential and your ability to grow and change because no one else will do it for you. You are just not there…yet.

For now, I just ask you to remain open to your growth and consider where you are at with your mindset. Do you see your failures as part of your identity or as something you can learn from? Do you believe in your potential to grow? I want to assume that you are someone who believes in your ability to grow and change, or else you may not have picked up this book, but I could be wrong.

Power

In her book, *Presence,* Dr. Amy Cuddy discusses two different types of power – personal power and social power. She says this about personal power:

> Personal power is characterized by freedom *from* the dominance of others. It is infinite, as opposed to zero-sum — it's about access to and control of limitless *inner* resources, such as our skills and abilities, our deeply held values, our true personalities, our boldest selves. Personal power allows us to shed the fears and inhibitions that prevent us from fully connecting with ourselves — with our beliefs, feelings, and skills.[11]

Yes and amen! When we feel powerless, like we have no control over ourselves, our growth is impeded. We can feel as though we are a victim of the circumstances around us. But, when we can take back our sense of control and power, we can become more present, more integrated versions of ourselves. I want you to move forward from this liminal season with a stronger sense of self and a renewed confidence in that self. We are here to take back our personal power.

Dr. Cuddy reiterates in her book that personal power is infinite, and it cannot be taken from us. It is all about accessing the resources that lie within you and believing that what you have to offer is worth pursuing. And the best part? Your personal power is not threatened when someone else finds theirs because no one else has your unique power. That truth alone helps me feel confident! You can't touch my power! And I don't have to think twice before I celebrate yours! With a focus on personal power, we all have limitless potential.

We cannot have personal power if we don't know where it comes from, though. We must be aware of what our defining skills, beliefs, and values are. Particularly in this time of unknown, you might be feeling more unsure or confused than ever on what all these pieces of you are. That's okay. That's why we are here. To do this work and discover who you are so you can feel more personally powerful.

I am someone who struggles greatly with needing a sense of control to feel powerful and happy. And through circumstances like the Covid-19 pandemic, the Universe humbly showed me how little control I actually have. Control is such an illusion when you really think about it. There are so few things we can control in our lives, but one thing I fully believe we can control is this idea of personal power because it comes from within. I believe God wants you to feel like you have some control, maybe not over every outcome, but over how you show up to everything that happens. God wants you to feel powerful in the face of liminal seasons. When you feel out of control, God doesn't want you to just sit back and wait until the Universe decides when the hard stuff will be over. We can take back our personal power and seize what control we do have. And one thing we can control is how we speak to ourselves and what beliefs we instill in ourselves.

Self-Belief

Coupled with your beliefs about God are your beliefs about yourself. This is equally as important in your self-discovery journey. Suppose we believe that God wants what is best for us but that we don't have the potential to get there. In that case, we will have a challenging time discovering, honoring, and owning our most authentic selves. So let's dive into a little psychology.

The Bandura Self-Efficacy Theory states that "self-efficacy is built on one's beliefs in the likelihood of future success; those who believe they have the ability to influence the events of their lives have high self-efficacy, while those who feel they are not in control and have little to no impact on what will happen to them in the future have low self-efficacy."[12] Self-efficacy is essential to a growth mindset in that it describes how much you believe you are in control of your ideal future. It also goes hand in hand with self-confidence, which we will touch on later.

It is critical here that you believe you have the power and ability to influence your future and make choices. Again, if you don't think you have any say over what happens, you will not take advantage of this time to grow. You have power here. You must believe you are a co-creator with God, and you have agency over the next steps your life takes. I say "must" because it's not something that can be compromised on this self-discovery journey. **We have to believe that the choices we make matter.**

It's important to be mindful of the language you use when talking to yourself. Be on the lookout for self-limiting beliefs such as statements that begin with "I can't, I don't, I'm not." We need expansive, hopeful language here. When our self-efficacy is low, we do not believe that our actions or choices matter because we don't believe we are in control. Therefore, we will be more likely to speak limiting beliefs over ourselves and maintain a fixed mindset. This might sound like, "I can't do this. What does it matter anyway? I'm not good enough. I'm not worth this effort." Stay kind to yourself and remember that no one starts their journey perfecting something new. At some point, you have to start before you are ready.

To combat self-limiting beliefs and help solidify that growth mindset, we need to have unshakeable truths about ourselves that we can cling to when our inner voice becomes critical. These are statements we can return to so we can boost our personal power and remind ourselves of the amazing humans we are. You were created with badassery in your bones. Sometimes we just forget it's there. So, I want you to come up with at least five unshakeable truths that you will cling to and believe in throughout this liminal time. Some of them can be about the Universe, and some can be about you. You pick the blend that works best for you, but I want you to write these with confidence in what you are saying. Then, I want you to write these on your mirror, on sticky notes, wherever you need them to be so you are reminded of them daily and often. And I'm not going to ask you to do anything that I won't also do, so I want to share some of my unshakeable truths with you here:

I am worthy of my dreams.

I am wrapped in a sacred, heated blanket of love and grace, no matter what I achieve.

I have unique gifts and strengths I offer this world.

I am complete right now, as I am.

Now I want you to write your own. Take some time and think them through. These are your guiding statements moving forward. Cultivating a strong sense of self-efficacy will only lead to more personal power and a compassionate growth mindset.

Once you begin to feel more personally powerful and in some control of your life again, you will find yourself making progress on your growth. I believe the fact that you purchased this book already reflects your decision to take back some personal power. You are in this unknown season, feeling stuck, and YOU decided to buy a resource that will (hopefully) help you develop and grow in this time. You took back the power. You said, "I am tired of feeling helpless and as though my life is fully out of my control." You said, "I want to become a better version of myself." You said, "I want to discover my most authentic self and come out of this unknown, potentially scary season, stronger than when I started." That's you owning your personal power and the choices you can make that honor that, so congrats! Be encouraged! This is already a huge step.

There is a lot of growth and change that can happen during this unknown season of life. Believing we have agency over what changes occur makes a significant difference in our lives. When you are confident in what you can bring to the table, then you will feel powerful. You will feel in control because your power will not be dependent on anyone else but you. And remember, the source of this power is infinite, so no one will be able to take it from you. No matter what happens moving forward, you've got the power.

Start Here:

1. Do you believe you currently hold a fixed or growth mindset? Why?
2. How do you define success?
3. How do you currently speak to yourself about the situation you are in? Are you kind or harsh? Do you blame yourself or are you gracious?
4. How are you hoping to grow in this season? What is the first baby step you could take toward that growth?
5. What is one unshakeable truth you want to believe more about yourself? What do you need to hear to boost your belief in yourself?

4

Stop the Should

HAVE YOU EVER TRIED TO plan a wedding during a global pandemic? Yeah, me either. Funny how the Universe likes to throw new challenges your way when you want them the least. For me, the whole wedding planning process was incredibly stressful even before the pandemic hit. By the time it was all said and done, I had planned our wedding three different times. And each time I planned it, I became more aware of how silly all the expectations of a perfect wedding truly are.

Wedding planning doesn't have to be this stressful season of emotion, but Instagram, blogs, and Pinterest really make brides feel guilty who aren't overwhelmed by all the minute details. My husband and I chose to get married in Austin, Texas, which is my hometown, but apparently also the hottest destination wedding location. It took us forever to find an available date and venue that was not astronomically over our budget. Once we secured the venue, there was a laundry list of to-dos to keep working on. I was so overwhelmed and felt insecure about every decision I made. As I began to feel more pressure, I started outsourcing every decision, always looking to others to tell me what to do. Yet what started out as a healthy source of inspiration quickly turned into an unhealthy amount of pressure to be perfect.

Between being a people-pleaser and a perfectionist, the wedding planning process drained me of a lot of joy. I felt so much pressure to do things a certain way. I wanted it to be the "perfect" day, not just for me but more so for my guests. I didn't want them to come to my wedding and have anything short of the best time. I worried about everyone's expectations but my own. The stress was sucking the life out of me and destroying the joy of this exciting season. Therefore, my therapist became my greatest resource during this time.

One day during our session, I was venting to my counselor about all the things I should do for the wedding - how I should get certain things done at a certain time, how I should do it all a certain way to please certain people, and who I should even invite. I was overwhelmed, exhausted, and frustrated. There were moments when the expectations for the wedding felt like so much that I wished we had just eloped! After I caught my breath and finished venting, my therapist paused, looked at me, and asked me a simple question. She asked, "Meredith, what should are you listening to?"

And just like that, the tears started to fall. The volcano of emotion began to erupt as my therapist asked me this earth-shattering question. In that moment, I realized I was listening to everyone else but myself.

The Source of the Should

We all listen to multiple sources of expectation when it comes to making decisions. I like to refer to those expectations, spoken or unspoken, as the "shoulds" of life. We look at the rest of the world and think our lives should look that way because that's what the standard is. And during seasons of liminality, we are even more prone to look outside of ourselves for answers than within. When we're feeling lost, we want direction, and it is hard to trust ourselves when we don't even know who we are. This insecurity leaves the door wide open for the "shoulds" of everyone else. Well, I don't know about you, but I was ready to stop shoulding myself.

The source of our "shoulds" are based in what psychologists call the social comparison theory, which says that our self-worth is based on how we measure against others.[13] This is when we feel like we should do something because someone else is doing it or has done it a certain way. While that can sometimes be a good, healthy source of motivation, it can also become toxic when others always define your why.

In her blog, life coach Jessi Kneeland defines "shoulding" as when you "create a ton of pressure on yourself to do or be something, based on what you think you're supposed to do or be, rather than on who you are and what you want."[14] With the weight of the "should" comes pressure to perform in a way that most likely isn't even true to our authentic selves. Before we know it, we get lost in making choices for our lives based on others rather than ourselves. In the liminal, unknown space you are currently in, it will be easy and tempting to just do or become what others think you "should" be. My goal is to help you discover your truest self and have the confidence to then own that best self as you move forward into the next season of your life. I hope to help you take advantage of this unknown space so you emerge from it knowing who you truly are, not who others think you should be. It is hard not to base our worth on others' expectations, so stay patient with yourself if this transformation does not happen overnight.

The first step in letting go of the "shoulds" in our lives is identifying their source. I believe there are three primary sources of our "shoulds" that we can feel trapped by, especially during times of transition. They are our peers, our parents, and our pride.

Peers

I really do think Instagram is of the devil sometimes. I can distinctly remember how happy and relieved I was the day that Instagram removed the number of likes from a post. That alone, the numerical counting of how many likes you got compared to someone else, was enough to crush anyone as they bravely shared an image or message on Instagram. It made me feel like if I didn't hit a certain number, then the post wasn't good enough, meaning I wasn't good enough. And if my friend and I posted the same picture, but one of us got more likes than the other? Game over. I definitely felt like I was doing something wrong.

Social media has created a way for us to stack our best versions of ourselves against one another to see who has more likes, comments, praise, attention, and overall validation. We know that people don't show the reality of what is going on through their social media. As they say, we are comparing highlight reels here! What we see on others' feeds isn't even a healthy or adequate measuring stick. So why do we do it? Why are we so quick to compare ourselves with our peers to establish our worth or figure out where we should be, particularly in this liminal season of life? I want us to recall the social comparison theory that I briefly mentioned before.

When it comes to "shoulding" ourselves in relation to our peers, we engage in social comparison. There are two types of social comparison, upward and downward. Kendra Cherry, a contributor to the website *Very Well Mind*, describes these two types of comparison. She writes, "People compare themselves to those who are better when they want inspiration to improve, and they compare themselves to those who are worse when they want to feel better about themselves."[15] I would argue that both upward and downward social comparison have the potential to be hurtful. We don't want to justify where we are in life by putting others down, and we don't want to push ourselves into guilt for not being where someone else is.

Upward comparison can be harmful or healthy. It is all dependent on your frame of mind when you unlock that phone and start scrolling through social media. There is a difference in looking at a peer who is achieving something that you genuinely also wish to work toward versus a peer who is doing something that you feel like you should do just because you're lost, and you want to be more like someone else. Motivation matters here, and security in your sense of self is critical to healthy upward comparison.

Is it too cheesy for me to say that where you're at today is enough? That being in a liminal time of transition is okay? And the people who don't own up to those transitional spaces and who aren't real about it aren't telling you the whole truth? Oops. Yeah, I said that. Everyone goes through unknown seasons at some point in life. Remember that the next time you hop on Instagram and think everyone has their stuff figured out but you.

It is critical that in this transitional time, you establish your sense of self-belonging. You cannot give others the power to determine your worth, and you cannot look to your peers as your measuring stick all the time. There is no perfect timeline. There is no "should" coming from the Universe about where you have to be. It's okay if you need time to discover who you are. It is good to use others for healthy inspiration, but it is harmful when you begin to give them power over how you feel about where you currently are in life.

I want you, as you are reading these words right now, to take a big deep breath with me, and as you exhale, I want you to say, "Where I'm at is where I'm supposed to be." We have to trust that. You don't need to look to others to validate if you are "doing it right." As you begin to really know yourself, you will begin to trust yourself. That's what this whole, messy, liminal season of life is about. The opportunity to discover who YOU are and what YOU want without the standard being set by anyone else, not even your parents or your family.

Parents

I'm an only child, which could imply many things for you as you read that, depending on your impression of only children. Yes, all the attention from my parents has been on me my whole life, but don't get confused and think this means I'm a spoiled brat…because we only children get a bad reputation for that. What did come from being an only child, though, was a lot of unspoken pressure on me to perform a certain way.

I can remember this one moment like it was yesterday. I was in fourth grade, and it was our end-of-the-year awards ceremony. My mom got me all dressed up, and I sat in the front row with my other classmates. They announced each award one by one and handed out paper certificates as prizes for them. After already winning awards like "Great at Spanish" or "Good Colorer," it was time for their biggest award – The Citizenship Award. This one wasn't about grades or talent, but it was about being a good person, helping your friends, and being kind to those around you. Well, I won the Citizenship Award, and I swear my mom reacted like I had won the Nobel Peace Prize at nine-years-old. We took that paper certificate home and framed it. Heck, I'm sure she still has it somewhere! This was the first time I can remember how good it felt to make my parents proud and how I just wanted more of that for the rest of my life.

For most of us, making our parents or our parental figures in our lives proud is meaningful and important. And, more often than not, making them proud means doing what they think we should do. Whether spoken or unspoken, our parents' expectations and their "shoulds" are powerful influencers on our behavior. Particularly, the unspoken "shoulds" can be the most painful and hard to identify. You want to make them proud, but you can't seem to ever get it right. There is this unspoken standard you are supposed to be meeting. Talk about pressure!

Some parents literally tell their children what they should or should not do. You know, it goes something like, "Oh, Melissa, you should really study business because that's the only way you'll have a steady, solid salary." Or "Oh, Jackie, you should definitely marry him because you don't know if you'll find someone else as good." Our families want what is best for us, but just like us, they can't predict the future or know what is actually best. Of course, everyone's relationships with their parents are different, and everyone's parents and family structures are different. But whether it's your parents, grandparents, mentors, or whoever fills this role in your life, you want to make them proud. They have this sense of authority in your life, so you want to lean on them for advice without having them dictate your life.

And, as I said, sometimes the unspoken "should" is worse than the vocal one. At least then you know what they expect of you. But with the unspoken "shoulds" that come out in nonverbal language or distancing or silent disapproval, you are just left guessing and frustrated as to what is actually pissing them off. So, how do we still show respect to the people in our lives who hold this sense of authority when we disagree with what they think is best for us? As a young person, how do you cope with the pressure from your parents to be perfect?

I believe it is all about self-discovery and self-love. When you begin to discover your truest self, you will want to honor that person. When you truly love yourself, you will make choices that reflect your most authentic self, and you will no longer need approval from those you admire. **You must get to a place where your love for yourself is greater than your need for approval from someone else.** No paper certificate will be given to you for loving who you are, but knowing and honoring your needs is the greatest prize any of us could receive. You will feel complete knowing that you are making choices that align with who you are so you can thrive. And you will not need anyone's praise, not even your parents, to make you feel like this work is worthwhile.

Pride

The final source of the "should" is our pride. Ah yes, even our own selves play a part in the "shoulds" of liminal space. When I reflect on this idea of pride and what we "should" deserve, I think about my freshman year of college and the serving of humble pie I received. See, in high school, I knew where I stood against everyone else, and I knew I had social status. Captain of the dance team? Nailed it. Solid friend group? You bet. Prom Queen? Hell yeah! Did I have a date to prom? No…but somehow, I still won! I guess all the boys were just intimidated by me, or at least that's what I told myself. Anyway, I graduated from high school feeling unstoppable, like I was the best of the best, and college would be a breeze.

But, to my surprise, college was not a breeze. When I arrived at college, I didn't even think that everyone else was also the cream of the crop at their high school. There were significantly more people competing for the same opportunities as me. But I didn't let that stop me! I still thought I would get everything I wanted. Within my first three months of college, I think I applied for eight different organizations or clubs and was only admitted to one. I would ask my friends how things worked out for them, and they'd respond with, "Oh yeah! I'm a tour guide! Oh…are you not? I'm so sorry." And then my pride would smack me in the face. I thought I should get all these opportunities because I was so amazing and deserved them. Well, I was WRONG. I was not hot shit anymore, and it was a good thing. Hello, real world.

Your pride might be tempted to talk to you and tell you where you should be in life right now. Your skills, education, and talents should be taking you somewhere else. You didn't deserve to get laid off. You didn't deserve to be broken up with. You didn't deserve to get sick. Trust me, I'm there with you, and this is not me trying to say otherwise. It doesn't matter whether you did or did not deserve whatever it is that sent you into the unknown because the reality is that you're here now. So you have a choice. Are you going to spend this time caught up in your pride about how you shouldn't be here? Or will you flip the script and lean into gratitude for this season? It's time to humble ourselves and surrender to our current reality. Until you open your closed fists that are shaking at God to receive what this season has to offer, you will never grow through it. Now you won't get praise for doing this self-work because internal reflection gets no applause. But the key to letting go of the "should" of our pride is to recognize where God has you and see it as a gift. **You must let go of where your pride thinks you should be and accept where you are at.**

Moving to Acceptance

How do we make this flip? How do we turn our pride into humility? Our frustration into gratitude? The first thing I want to remind you to do is to FEEL. No matter how you found yourself in this season of liminality, it started with a loss, and I don't want you to rush past that. You have to feel before you can heal, so if you haven't done so already, cry, cuss, yell into your pillow, do whatever you need to so you can grieve the loss of the old. Once you're in a clearer emotional state, we can begin the flipping. We can begin to believe that what we have in this unknown is enough. We can start to move toward gratitude, receive the gift of this time, and be open to what we will discover. But we must first release the pressure we are putting on ourselves to be somewhere else or the resentment we feel that got us here. Because here we are. We must surrender to the now.

Gratitude practices can be extremely powerful in helping us accept where we are, especially if it is somewhere we'd rather not be. One of my favorite sayings is that "gratitude turns what we have into enough." **When we are unsure of what's coming next, grounding ourselves in gratitude will help us stay present and appreciate the in-between time.** These practices do not have to be complicated. You might consider writing down three things you are grateful for at the end of each day. Or you could text a friend what you are thankful for so you can share it with someone else.

A practice that has been very helpful for me over the years is keeping a gratitude calendar. I just get a big wall calendar for the year, hang it somewhere I will see it daily, and write down one thing I'm grateful for each day on the date. As time passes, the calendar becomes filled with gratitude, and I can reflect on what gifts that month gave me. It evolves into this beautiful piece of art, helping me visualize all I am grateful for. And it reminds me, especially in times where my pride wants to tell me I should be elsewhere, that right here is where I am supposed to be. There is good in the now. There is growth in the now. Gratitude helps me remember that each day. So if you feel especially stuck with this "should," I highly recommend starting a gratitude practice to help cultivate an open mindset. The benefits of gratitude are endless, so why not start now.

Identify Your "Shoulds"

I want you to take some time and identify what the source of the "shoulds" are in your life. Is it your peers, your pride, or your parents?

It might be a combination of them or none at all, but it is essential to know where your "shoulds" are currently coming from so we know how to identify them and move past them.

I'm going to introduce to you an activity that has helped me immensely in this process. I encourage you to get out your journal or paper and do this with me. We are going to name the "should" statements we are believing and why. For example, regarding my wedding planning pressure, a statement I believed was: I should create a beautiful, floral wedding ceremony because all the wedding blogs set an extraordinary standard to be met. I simply wrote what I believed I should do and why. From there, I was able to determine where that "should" was coming from and eliminated it moving forward. The template is simple. It's just:

I should _____ because _____.

Give it a try. Sit with yourself for at least five minutes and ask yourself the tough questions. What do you feel like you should do in this time and why? What do you feel like your next step should be and why? Be patient with yourself as you do this work. The first step before any change is to build awareness surrounding where we currently are.

Start Here:

1. Where is you loudest "should" coming from?
2. In what areas of your life do you not trust yourself?
3. Where do you feel restless and eager to outsource decisions?
4. Who do you compare yourself to? Is this upward or downward comparison? Why?
5. How can you flip your perspective and see this unknown time as an opportunity? What might you be grateful for?

5

WHO YOU ARE

NOW THAT WE HAVE DETERMINED and examined where the source of your expectations is coming from, we can replace it with what is most true for you. As a refresher, I want to circle back to Jessi Kneeland's definition of "shoulding." She writes that "shoulding" is when you "create a ton of pressure on yourself to do or be something, based on what you think you're supposed to do or be, rather than on who you are and what you want." We will unpack these last two statements in these next two chapters and help you figure out what really should be the source of your decisions. Instead of letting outside expectations guide us, we will learn how to trust our authentic selves in decision-making. I believe this can be broken down into three main categories for our lives: our needs, values, and dreams.

Needs

Everyone has basic needs that have to be met, like food, clothing, and water. But beyond that, I want you to know yourself so well that you know what you need to succeed in whatever comes next for you. I want you to know how to take care of your basic needs and how to protect yourself from the influence of others when they try and challenge what you need. Only you know what is best for you.

You might be familiar with Maslow's Hierarchy of Needs, but if you are not, it is this handy little pyramid in the world of psychology that breaks down our needs in order of importance. Like a food pyramid, the most substantial, basic needs must be met by all people to survive. So, these needs are represented as the pyramid's foundation at the bottom. As the pyramid gets smaller at the top, fewer people have the opportunity to fulfill those needs in their lives. There are five total levels of needs in Maslow's Hierarchy, so let's break them down.

The first level of Maslow's Hierarchy is our physiological needs. These are the basic survival needs like food, water, shelter, and sleep. This base level of need can be easy to skip over because we might assume these demands will get taken care of. Of course, I trust that you fulfill these needs when they arise because you literally will not be able to function without them. Still, it is essential to think about what the need is and how it is being met. These needs are the foundation that fuels our lives, so we mustn't let them fall to the bottom of our priority list. And the basic need that almost everyone prioritizes last? Yup, you guessed it. Sleep.

According to the American Sleep Apnea Association, sleep problems in America are pervasive, with 70% of adults reporting that they obtain insufficient sleep at least one night a month, and 11% reporting insufficient sleep every night.[16] Apparently, a lot of us think we're invincible, but we will not be able to function in this world without sleep. Insufficient sleep affects proper brain functioning, too, and I don't know about you, but I would prefer my brain to be working with its maximum potential. In their book, *Burnout: The Secret to Unlocking the Stress Cycle,* Dr. Emily Nagoski and Amelia Nagoski share, "We were built to oscillate between wakefulness and sleep, because we require the things our brain does on its own during sleep to make us fully functional while we're awake."[17] We can't move through the world as fully functioning humans if we do not get the sleep our bodies need. And with 11% of adults stating that they don't get adequate sleep every night, we have a big problem on our hands and a lot of half-alive humans trying to make it in this world. If you've been in college, then you probably have had the experience of your body shutting down on you as a result of a lack of sleep. You know it's not fun. Long story short: inadequate sleep = inadequate functioning.

We have to prioritize rest. There is no arguing against it. And while sleep is the most prominent facet of rest that most of us neglect, we need to be mindful of other kinds of rest, as well. In her book,

Sacred Rest, Dr. Saundra Dalton-Smith names the seven types of rest you need to feel fully recharged: physical, mental, social, creative, emotional, spiritual, and sensory rest.[18] With this in mind, rest means more than just sleep! Our brains need a break, too, so instead of always reading for intellectual stimulation, maybe you pick up a fiction book or just let your mind wander for a day. Perhaps you flex that creative muscle and write for fun or enjoy listening to one of your favorite albums. Social rest might mean you intentionally say no to plans with friends so you can unwind and reconnect with yourself. Or, maybe the opposite, perhaps some time with loved ones is the social rest you need to stimulate love and reconnection. Sleep is foundational, and all rest is essential. Remember, this is the most significant chunk of our pyramid of needs, so do not skip this step. Focus on your foundation, then the rest will follow.

The second level of our pyramid of needs is our safety and security needs, such as emotional, financial, and physical safety. Before you can grow, you need to feel safe and secure in your space of belonging. Financially, you have to provide your basic needs first, which might mean focusing on getting stable before you can dream a little bigger. You might not be in a place where you can explore your options for jobs to the extent you wish you could right now because you need to get food on the table or pay rent. Please don't throw this book in the trash if that is you. Prioritize getting secure first. Provide this basic need. Then dig deeper into self-discovery. Just because you accept a job for the sake of money now doesn't mean that this work will not serve you in your next step.

We can learn from every single experience. Hear me when I say that I recognize this internal work is a privilege. Like Maslow's pyramid, it gets smaller at the top because fewer people have the freedom to be in a place where they can self-actualize. More people are in the place where they need to be safe and secure. So do not feel guilty or discouraged if this is where you are. Do what you need to do to prioritize this need.

Third, we have to fulfill our need for love and belonging. This pyramid level is rooted in the importance of relationships and how we were not made to do life alone. Starting in childhood, we crave connection with our parents, and from there on out, we don't stop! Notice that this level is not simply described as relationships but also love and belonging. We all need those communities and people in our lives where we can feel wholly known and loved for exactly who we are. The Nagoski sisters call this concept of love and belonging the "Bubble of Love," which has two primary ingredients: trust and connected knowing.[19]

Trust is required to feel like you can be your authentic self with someone else. If you don't trust them, you will be hesitant to open up, be vulnerable, and be honest with them. Trust boils down to one question, "Are you there for me?"[20] Especially as you are stepping out of a season of uncertainty into something you've never experienced before, you need these people you can share your honest thoughts, experiences, and dreams with. They can only help you achieve them if they know about them.

Connected knowing is when you understand something or, rather, someone by getting to know them in their own context. You aren't separating their lived experience or life from the context they know. You are building empathy with them, seeking to understand who they are in the context they are in, not your own. This isn't about acceptance but about wanting to understand their point of view and their authentic self. If, as someone is sharing, we try and correct them or change them, then that person probably won't feel like they can trust us or are very connected to us. Again, building trust and having a Bubble of Love is about love and belonging. If we aren't willing to empathize and listen to the other person, they won't feel seen or belong.

As we intimately get to know others without judgment, we can begin to do the same for ourselves. Knowing others in their contexts is like holding up a mirror to our own lives to more closely understand ourselves from a different perspective. We all need love and belonging to thrive and feel supported. Whether that's with a romantic partner, a best friend, parents, or a team, let yourself be vulnerable and authentically connect with someone you trust. Let them in and watch yourself grow.

Next are our esteem needs, which come in two different forms, esteem for oneself and the desire for reputation or respect from others.[21] According to Maslow, we need to feel confident in our ability to master skills and achieve goals independently of others, and we also need to be recognized by others for our hard work. Building self-esteem comes as we reach more goals and dreams. With your foundational needs met and a sense of love and belonging, you will have the support you need to actually begin achieving the things you set out to do! As you start to demonstrate ability and achievement in what matters to you, your self-esteem will continue to grow.[22] The final level of needs is self-actualization, where the need is to meet one's fullest potential as an individual. You will want to experience all the personal growth you can and become the most ideal version of yourself at this level of need. This is you chasing after your dreams and believing you have what it takes to achieve them. This is you confidently taking your next step toward what you really want while honoring who you authentically are.

You might be both at the self-actualization stage and in a season of liminality. That is very possible! But, for most people navigating transition, I would say they probably land somewhere between levels two-four. Your basic needs are met, and now you have to discover how to feel secure in your circumstances, love yourself and others, and develop your self-esteem. I encourage you to determine what level of Maslow's Hierarchy you think you're at, as it will help you know what to prioritize in this current season of life.

When you identify what you need, whether that is more sleep, more water, more honest love, more recognition, or anything else, you have to prioritize it. And this frequently looks like setting clear boundaries. This applies to all of Maslow's Hierarchy of Needs because when we allow others to dictate how we should live our lives, we give them power over how we care for our needs. It is essential you learn to set and protect a boundary with any need. I love how Dr. Dalton-Smith speaks of these boundaries:

A life secured by personal boundaries is confident and resonates with your values. It is energized by your choices and aligns with your priorities. Boundaries in rest relate to understanding the reasons behind every yes and what differentiates a yes within your boundaries from one outside of your boundaries. **Any yes given out of fear, shame, guilt, or insecurity should be a no**...Your boundary lifelines are reinforced when you define your limitations and accept the truth about what is needed to restore and revive your life. It is healthy to prioritize your personal needs, sometimes even over the needs of those you care for. **Don't expect others to give you permission to take care of yourself.** Know what is required for you to put your best self out there to do the things you were meant to do, and be bold in guarding your life against invasion.[23]

Only when you take care of these basic needs will you be in a healthy place to consider your best next step as you emerge from this liminal season. Like Dr. Dalton-Smith says, others will not give you permission to do what you need to do to take care of yourself. Get well-acquainted with your needs in this season. First, your basic ones, and then move up the pyramid to what you need to feel secure, supported, and confident. And as you move up the pyramid, don't forget to set clear boundaries every step of the way.

Values

The next step in pushing back against the expectations of others in our lives is to identify our values. Your values are your core beliefs. They are your priorities that drive your "why" behind all you do. **We honor our most authentic selves when we live in alignment with our values.** A season of transition is a beautiful gift of time you can use to do this inner work. If you want to emerge as the freest, authentic version of yourself, you must consistently know and honor your values. Your values are your internal compass that guides the path to your most authentic self.[24] If you want to make better choices in your life, whether that be about what you have for dinner, who you date, or what job you accept, you have to know and honor your values. It is not enough to simply be aware of your values. You have to remind yourself of them regularly and assess whether you live in alignment with them. Often, things don't work out because they ultimately do not align with our values. If you want to make decisions that will last for the long run, you need to clarify what matters most to you.

Discovering and naming our values can be challenging, though. It's hard work that doesn't always happen overnight. Some of you might be able to look at a list and know immediately, or others might need days and weeks to reflect and think through it. We'll talk through how to evaluate your values in whatever way serves you best. This isn't a race, so don't worry if it takes you a little while to get clear on them.

In her chapter on values in *Dare to Lead,* Dr. Brené Brown writes, "Living into our values means that we do more than profess our values, we practice them. We walk our talk – we are clear about what we believe and hold important, and we take care that our intentions, words, thoughts, and behavior align with those beliefs."[25] We must clarify our values if we hope to live lives in alignment with them. Dr. Brown believes that there is only one set of values each of us has that apply to every situation.[26] We cannot separate work values from personal values if we want to live an authentic life – they all come together and are part of who we are. It is essential to get clear on your values so you know what decisions to make that help you live according to them.

To help you get started, it can be helpful to have a list of values to peruse for inspiration. Literally, you can google "list of values," and I'm sure a bunch will pop up. Then, begin to identify which ones resonate with you. Again, this doesn't have to be an activity you do in one sitting. You might need to pick a handful of values, marinate on them for a few days, and see how they really show up for you in your life and desired behaviors. Dr. Brown recommends selecting two core values so you can actually honor them well. If we have closer to ten or fifteen values, then it can become just a list of feel-good words and not actually what grounds our life choices or decisions.[27]

A helpful set of questions that I used to narrow down my core values comes from psychologist Dr. Anna Rowley. She was in a conversation about anxiety held by the incredible women at Shine Text where she posed the questions: *What would my life be like without this value? What really makes my life meaningful? What are some characteristics or behaviors of role models I want to emulate?*[28]

So, let's say one of the values you are considering is calmness. Think about what your life would be like without it. How do you feel when you take prioritizing and protecting your sense of calm away? Do you still feel in alignment and whole? Or does it leave you feeling like something is missing, and you no longer live in integrity to what is most important to you? I loved asking myself these questions because it really helped me solidify my values. I discovered that my two core values are inclusion and gratitude from this exercise. All the other values I was considering stem from these two, so ultimately, I concluded that these values are at the core of all I do and want to be.

Alright, now it's your turn! Get googling and get considering. If you do this activity and still feel stuck or unsure of your values, try considering these other helpful tools. You can observe your daily choices with more curiosity, think about how those choices made you feel, and reflect on key moments in your life that stand out and why.[29] Take your time with this work. Living in alignment with your values is an incredible way to gain confidence as you move forward from this season of liminality. Because no matter how others may choose to judge your decisions, you will know they are right for you.

Once you've identified your values, I suggest writing or typing them out somewhere, so you are reminded of them daily. This could look like post-it notes, reminders on your phone, something in your car, or whatever you need to keep your values presently in front of you. With your values in places where you will see them, you will be continuously reminded of what you want to honor in your life and the person you want to become.[30] Once you have identified your core values, I also want you to share them with someone close to you for two reasons. I want you to feel recognized for the hard work you have done (level four of Maslow's Hierarchy, anyone?) and I want someone to hold you accountable for living into your values. Sometimes, this can get uncomfortable when you get called out for not living in alignment, but that is where the growth happens.

So friend, take the time to do these exercises to discover your values. Once you know them, share them, remind yourself of them however you need to, and hold yourself accountable to them every day. Evaluate how you're feeling and dig a little deeper to see if it might be because you are not honoring your core values. I am a work in progress on this, too, but when I actively am aware of my values, I can make better choices that help me live a life of meaning and joy.

Dreams

When was the last time you imagined the impossible for yourself? The last time you dreamed big? Let's be honest, college can kind of ruin your dreams if you aren't careful. Maybe you came into college wanting to study art history. Then you learned how prestigious the business school is and how all your friends were taking accounting in the fall, so before you knew it, you enrolled in BUSI 101. We can get distracted by what everyone else is doing really fast, and question if what we are studying is really what we "should" be doing. We begin waking up to our needs and realize that we have to actually make an income. Can we pursue our dream and survive? Is my dream worth all the work and discomfort? Sometimes after we graduate college and enter into the real world, we are so far gone that we forget how to dream altogether. If you've started to minimize your potential somewhere along the way, I want you to give yourself permission to dream again. Visualizing your dreams can help significantly with this. It can be uncomfortable to envision your ideal future or life, but it is in the discomfort where belief and change actually happen.

One day in Divinity School, I had a friend ask me, "Meredith if you had all the money in the world and an empty building, what would you do?" This question left me stunned because it was the first time in so long that someone had encouraged me to imagine and visualize a dream. Truly, a dream, because we all know the reality of time, money, and space is a challenge, but it's just dreaming y'all! You have permission to envision whatever you want. When my friend asked me this question, she asked me to engage with my imagination. The thing about dreams is…they haven't happened…yet. So, it's hard to sometimes really name them and know them unless we engage in our imagination and let ourselves go there first in our heads. If we believe that we are co-creators with God and have a say in this life we are living, then we can assume that God gave us this ability to imagine with purpose. **You are honoring what God wants for your life when you imagine the fullest possibilities for your life. God wants you to go after what YOU want!** God put those desires and dreams within you in the first place. It is honoring to God when you honor your dreams.

As you consider your goals for your life, is it too mystical of me to suggest that the Universe might even speak to you through your dreams? Roll with me here. I promise I'm not trying to get too Sigmund Freud on you. Have you ever considered that your dreams might serve a purpose? Wilkie and Noreen Cannon Au share that "when we pay attention to our dreams and actively work on them, we profess our belief that our inner life matters because it is the place where our treasure lies. Dreamwork builds a bridge between our ego and our soul, or between our waking self and our deepest self."[31] Our treasure lies within! Do you know how you get to buried treasure? You have to dig deep. You have to keep going down and inward to discover the gift that lies within. When we are unconscious in our sleep, we allow ourselves to go deeper than we ever could when awake. Don't discount the possibility that your dreams might be communicating your real-life goals to you. They are a beautiful tool for self-discovery that you can learn from during this time.

Suppose dreamwork as a self-discovery tool is not comfortable for you. In that case, I encourage another process of sinking deeper with meditation. When we get quiet and still, we can finally hear ourselves speak to us without the noise of the external world drowning our voices out. You can actually hear yourself say what you truly want. Mindfulness and meditation are two practices that have served me so well these past few years in moving past the muck of what others think and figuring out what I really want. Again, this could be as small as deciding what my body is actually hungry for dinner or as big as quitting a job because I feel more at peace with that decision than staying. Meditation might sound like something out of reach for you, but trust me, it just takes some practice, and you will be craving the silence and comforting rhythm of your breath. It feels good to give yourself the uninterrupted attention you deserve.

The World Needs YOU

Honoring your needs, values, and dreams matters because we want to replace the motivation for our behavior from what we "should" do to who we are and what we want. No matter what brought you to this time of transition, you will have decisions to make about who you will be on the other side. Friend, listen close. God created beautiful you with all your specific needs, values, and dreams built into your bones. The Universe has infused you with a gift no one else has. No one else can offer what you can. Jen Sincero says it this way in her book *You Are a Badass:*

> You are loved. Massively. Ferociously. Unconditionally.
> The Universe is totally freaking out about how awesome
> you are. It's got you wrapped in a warm gorilla hug of

adoration. It wants to give you everything you desire. It wants you to be happy. It wants you to see what it sees in you.

You are perfect. To think anything less is as pointless as a river thinking that it's got too many curves or that it moves too slowly or that its rapids are too rapid. Says who? You're on a journey with no defined beginning, middle or end. There are no wrong twists and turns. There is just being. **And your job is to be as you as you can be.** This is why you're here. To shy away from who you truly are would leave the world you-less. You are the only you there is and ever will be. I repeat, *you are the only you there is and ever will be.* Do not deny the world its one and only chance to bask in your brilliance.[32]

This all goes back to our unshakeable beliefs. Do you believe that the Universe wants you to be happy? Do you believe that God loves you unconditionally as you are? Do you believe you were made to be celebrated as your most authentic self? Do you believe you are perfect, just as you are?

We need you and your unique needs, values, and dreams in this world. Something is missing that only you can fill. And that will never happen if we live lives based on what others tell us we should do. They don't know you like you know you. You have to believe that you are worthy of a life that honors your authentic self. No more letting the "shoulds" of others dictate your life. You will burst out of this season of transition as the most honest version of yourself, not settling for anyone else's idea of what your life should be. Let's get to work.

Start Here:

1. What level of Maslow's Hierarchy of Needs are you at in this season? From there, what needs do you need to prioritize meeting first?
2. How can you advocate for the needs you must meet first right now? What changes might you need to make?
3. What are you two core values? How might you more effectively honor them in your decision-making?
4. What does it look like to honor your core values in your everyday life? In your career? In your relationships?
5. What is the biggest dream you have for your life? Close your eyes and dream big. There are NO limits here!

6

WHAT YOU WANT

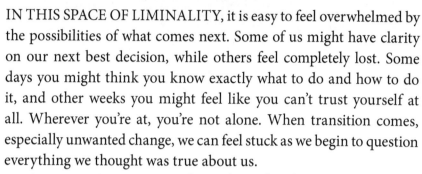

IN THIS SPACE OF LIMINALITY, it is easy to feel overwhelmed by the possibilities of what comes next. Some of us might have clarity on our next best decision, while others feel completely lost. Some days you might think you know exactly what to do and how to do it, and other weeks you might feel like you can't trust yourself at all. Wherever you're at, you're not alone. When transition comes, especially unwanted change, we can feel stuck as we begin to question everything we thought was true about us.

As we are in a season of searching for the next decision, it is entirely healthy and natural to want to keep exploring your vocation. **Exploration and curiosity are vital to transforming our perspective on liminality.** We can acknowledge that this season is hard and maybe not what we wanted but that it could also actually be good for us. It gives us space to re-evaluate the direction we thought we were heading in for one that serves us better. And, whether we like it or not, our career does help shape and define a lot of who we are and what we want, so it is essential to think through our vocation.

So what is vocation anyway? It sounds like this fancy spiritual word, but all it means is your calling. Parker Palmer defines it this way:

> Today I understand vocation quite differently – not as a goal to be achieved but as a gift to be received. Discovering vocation does not mean scrambling toward some prize just beyond my reach but accepting the treasure of true self I already possess. Vocation does not come from a voice 'out there' calling me to become something I am not. It comes

from a voice 'in here' calling me to be the person I was born to be, to fulfill the original selfhood given me at birth by God.[33]

I absolutely love this reframing of vocation. We weren't supposed to discover our calling outside of ourselves in the first place! Now you have this gift of time and space to connect with your innermost, authentic self and let it speak to you. Instead of looking outside yourself for validation or direction, you can look within for the answers.

Our vocation is ever evolving. Just because you decide to pursue a certain career path now does not mean that it can't change in the future. Where we start doesn't always have to be where we finish. We must honor the ways we change and grow with a vocation that does the same. Quitting a job does not mean you failed. Trying something and learning you don't like it isn't a waste of time. Every season and every opportunity has its purpose. It's totally okay to change your job. It's okay to go back to school. It's normal to not know exactly what you want to do.

Discovering your truest self is the best gift this season of liminality can give you. God created you with unique dreams and gifts already within you, but too many of us let the world dictate who we become without realizing it. We never pause to evaluate if our choices are really in alignment with our most authentic self – our needs, values, and dreams. We don't take time to discover the gifts we offer inwardly, so we stick to the status quo. In our world, it is tempting to be identified by what we do rather than who we are, but what if we allowed who we truly are to determine what we do?

I have had a very non-linear vocational path with plenty of liminal, transitional space. Typically, during these times of transition and discovery, I would feel this surge of shame for not having it "figured out." Hence, me writing this book so you know that you are not alone. It is totally normal to not have it all go according to plan or to have your life look different than how you envisioned it. We want to rush through uncertain seasons as fast as possible, so we have something to show the world, to prove to them that we are okay and capable and worthy. But I want you and me both to slow down, and to not miss what God wants to reveal to us during this time. I would argue that everyone needs to embrace transition and unknowing seasons more to discover what they don't already know about themselves.

Sometimes, we find ourselves in these liminal spaces without knowing what to do next. It can sometimes feel overwhelming if you genuinely don't know where to begin. Our vocational dreams can be hard to identify at times, which is why there are so many tools and professionals out there helping folks find their path. If you're stuck, you are also not alone. As with anything that feels overwhelming at first, it can be most helpful to break it down into smaller steps and start simple. You might start by asking yourself, "What do I like to do?"

How Do I Know What I Like?

One of my friends called me the other day because she is in-between jobs but doesn't know what to pursue next. She shared with me that when she sought help, a mentor in her life simply asked her what she liked. So, my friend began to list what she enjoyed doing, googled those things, and within an hour, found a one-year graduate school program in a city she loves that feels like the perfect next step for her. So, why not try starting there if you're stuck! What do you like? Google it! Just search, research, and explore what's out there. You never know what you might find.

To discover what you genuinely like, you also have to let yourself be bored. I know I know; God forbid I ask you to be bored and not run to your phone or Netflix for instant distraction or gratification. Our generation is glued to our phones, whether we want to admit it or not. While there are many gifts in being connected all the time, it prevents us from discovering our talents and dreams when we are always looking at others and not taking time to be reflective with ourselves. When we are bored and don't run to our phones for distraction, we are forced to discover what else we want to do. Do you want to write? Play music? Run? Cook? Who knows! But I know you won't know what you genuinely gravitate to or like to do if you always fill your voids of boredom with other people's lives. This journey is about discovering your OWN self! On boredom, Glennon Doyle says it best, "The moment after we don't know what to do with ourselves is the moment we find ourselves. Right after itchy boredom is self-discovery. But we have to hang in there long enough without bailing."[34] Let yourself be bored so you can give yourself a chance to discover what you love. Or, at the very least, what you like.

If you are completely stuck with not knowing what to pursue, my final suggestion is to take different personality/strengths assessments. There are plenty of ones on the Internet! Assessments like the Strong Interest Inventory, Enneagram, StrengthsQuest, and Myers-Briggs have all served me so well in helping me understand who I am, how I'm motivated, and how my interests align with certain vocations. These assessments can help you know yourself better and what you need in a role to feel fulfilled. For example, I am a two on the Enneagram, meaning I am a helper – I have to be in a position where I feel like I am helping others. Ideally, since I am also super extroverted according to Myers-Briggs, I need a highly relational helping profession. These tools helped me decide to pursue licensure in professional counseling. I particularly like the Enneagram because it reveals your why or driving motivation behind all you do. It will show both your good side and your dark side, which is helpful self-awareness for any season in life. On the Enneagram, Ian Morgan Cron writes:

> The purpose of the Enneagram is to develop self-knowledge and learn how to recognize and dis-identify with the parts of our personalities that limit us so we can be reunited with our truest and best selves, that 'pure diamond, blazing with the invisible light of heaven,' as Thomas Merton said. The point of it is self-understanding and growing beyond the

self-defeating dimensions of our personality, as well as improving relationships and growing in compassion for others.[35]

The more you get to know yourself, the more you will accurately identify what types of vocations fit you well and help you feel alive and fulfilled. When I took the Enneagram finder for the first time, I felt so exposed. I was blown away by how accurately it described every part of me, even my deepest, most insecure longings. It helps to feel this understood and seen, though. We have to acknowledge both the good and challenging parts of our personalities to find our best fits.

Get Curious

There is ample room to explore in your life. I think a myth many of us believe is that we must have our career "figured out" early on, and any detours we take are a waste of time. Absolutely not! Try not to get so caught up in knowing your one purpose or your one passion. Any setback is just part of your journey. **You will not miss your purpose in life**, so if you are filling your head with self-help podcasts and books (guilty as charged) with talk of needing to figure out your one thing, turn those off! It is completely normal to re-route and change directions at any time. I want to encourage us to get curious about what stirs in our hearts. What's that thing that has always interested you, but maybe you've been too scared or nervous to admit it? What's the urge you've wanted to explore? It is time to embrace curiosity, my friend. **You are co-creating with God every step of the way, and God put curiosities in your heart for a reason.**

Not only should you explore your interests, but I believe that exploring your feelings and potential opportunities will help you grow. In this season of liminality, it is beneficial to get curious about your feelings. When you feel sad, anxious, or frustrated, resist running to something else like your phone or food to numb or distract you from your uncomfortable feeling. Sit with it for a moment. Then, get curious. Ask yourself why you might be feeling this way. What triggered my anxiety? Where have my thoughts drifted? What did I do or not do today that might be leading me to feel this way? Why am I feeling sad at this moment? By asking yourself these why questions about your feelings, you can discover what is bringing you to those places of emotion, which can help you uncover certain truths about yourself. And when you discover the root cause of emotions like anger or love, you find out what really matters to you. Your passions are rooted in your feelings, so getting curious about them is a great starting point to discovering what you might want to do next.

Secondly, you might have new opportunities presented in this liminal season. These could be anything from a social gathering to a possible job to an online class. Anything! You might be browsing the Internet one day, and something could strike your interest. Do not let your fear of the unknown or your fear of failure stop you from getting curious about new opportunities. Facts are facts: if you say no to a new opportunity, you are guaranteed not to grow, but if you say yes, you are guaranteed to develop just by showing up in the first place. Think about it. Even if you don't feel like you gained anything from the opportunity, you develop your curiosity and bravery muscles by showing up even if you are a little scared. This will only serve you moving forward. You will not grow if you do not become curious about new things that spark your interest. So, let yourself explore!

Gifts

Finally, I want you to take inventory and consider what gifts you have to offer this world. Reflect on what you are already good at and think outside the box on how you might be able to lean into that gift more. Not only do I want you to be pursuing your passions and curiosities, but I want you to consider what natural skills you have. Coupling your gifts with your discoveries in curiosity will allow you to serve the world to your maximum extent.

This is also a great place to start if you are feeling stuck. What are you naturally good at? Do you write? Cook? Dance? It can be anything at all! Your gifts can serve you well as you move forward and consider your next step. And if you don't think you have any gifts, THINK AGAIN! God has equipped each of us with our unique offerings to embrace. **You have purpose built into your creation.** You have something special.

Dream vs Reality

Okay, let's say you get set on your dream. You've done some of this work, you know what you want to pursue, and you are energized to make it happen. Amazing! But then the hard truth of reality hits. You would love to pursue your vocational dream, but you need money to live! Reality CHECK. How do you do both? How do you honor and pursue your dream if you know that it won't provide what you need financially at this moment? How do you reconcile your very real needs with your vision?

Ah, friend, this is the big dilemma, isn't it! I want so badly to tell you to chase after your dream somewhat blindly, but this is the real world we live in, and we still need money to pay our bills. We have to be realistic about our dreams at some point, which is my least favorite part. I'm not here to deceive you or not recognize the hard truths we face as we want to go after our dreams, though. We must embrace reality.

Let's reconsider Maslow's Hierarchy. Our second level of need is safety and security. We must meet this need before moving up the pyramid to achieve esteem and self-actualization. In other words, yes, you need to have money to provide yourself the security you also need to pursue your dreams.

I do not want this to discourage you or stop you, though! The pursuit of our dreams looks different in every season of life. In this time of transition, while I do want you to zero in on what that dream might be for you, I also want to give you practical skills because I care that you meet your basic needs. Prioritization of your needs does not mean the dream has to go on hold. It might just look like a different amount of time or energy investment right now.

One of my favorite examples of balancing our needs with our dreams is Ellen's Stardust Diner in New York City. I went there for the first time in eighth grade when my mom and I took a trip to the Big Apple to celebrate my birthday. I remember walking in and being in total awe of the lights and over-the-top restaurant décor. What makes Ellen's Stardust Diner special is that all the waitstaff are singers, and at any moment during your dining experience, they could break out in song. And these singers are SO GOOD! Most of them are in New York City to pursue their dream of being on Broadway, but they might choose to work somewhere like Ellen's until they make it big. This way, they can continue to embody their passion for singing while making enough money to live. These individuals took a risk to move to a new city to pursue their dream, but they also do what they need to be secure.

What might your version of Ellen's Stardust Diner look like? One of my best friends is a full-time fitness instructor now, managing and leading other instructors and studios. They started as a part-time fitness instructor who also worked at another gym and lululemon to be financially secure. They did not let go of their vocational dream, though, and once they got promoted, they were able to let the other jobs go.

Commitment and hard work go a long way, especially when you don't see the results immediately. Dreams do not come with instant gratification. And to clarify again, I don't mean dream as some pie in the sky, fluffy "dream" for your life. I mean the vision of how you can honor that longing inside, that gift you have, that you want to share with the world. The dream that fulfills you and leaves you with a sense of alignment in all you do.

Don't box yourself in here and put your dream entirely on hold because it won't provide the level of need you are at now. There is purpose in every step of your journey, so do not discount your small beginning. **Don't deny yourself the opportunity to begin at all**

just because it might not look how you imagined it would. If it is important to you, you can get creative and find a way to start taking those steps toward that dream, no matter where you are at with your needs.

Vocation is a gift to be received, much like this time of liminality. It might take some work to determine your gifts, curiosities, strengths, and interests. When you do, you will be able to move forward into this next season of life with more certainty that you are honoring your authentic self. **To live a fulfilling life means living in accordance with who you are.** Don't rush the process of getting to know yourself. It will take a lifetime, but here and now, in the in-between, you can dive right in. As we learn more about ourselves and begin considering our next steps, we might be torn or unsure of the "right" decision. But here's the myth buster, there is no right decision, only the opportunity to learn from every decision.

Start Here:

1. Let yourself be bored. Then see what you gravitate to and reflect on the experience. What did you draw toward?
2. Do you know your Enneagram or Myers-Briggs score? Hop on the Internet and find out! Then take some time to reflect on what these insights help you learn about yourself and your potential vocation.
3. What are you curious to learn more about?
4. List some of the gifts you believe you have to offer the world.
5. What might be limiting you from pursuing your dream in the way you want to right now? How might you be able to adjust and continue to take steps toward it anyway?

7

DECISION MAKING

I WAS SO STUCK NOT knowing what career to pursue in college. Yeah, I liked my classes and the degree I was going after, but I still wasn't sure what the actual job would be. My bachelor's degrees are in psychology and religion. Not a super clear career path lined up for me with that combo. So, I used the resources at my university and visited the career center to take a test. After sifting through the plethora of questions, I finished and met with the counselor to walk me through my results. She showed me my strengths, interests, all these other things, and then got down to it – my top five careers. Number one was a speech pathologist, which many of my friends were studying to become. I did have a moment where I thought I might want to do this. Helping people improve their speech felt like a meaningful and important job! My number two career was a bartender. And number three? Nursing home administrator. Not the most exciting career to be told you'd be fit for at age twenty-one. All this to say, yes, it helped clarify things for me, but this test wasn't the decision-making factor in itself.

Without any clearer direction, I decided to keep taking what felt like the right next step for me at the time and hoped for the best. So far, it had worked out, but now we were talking about the real world. Could I trust my gut in this decision-making process, too? What if my heart had led me down the wrong path throughout college, and I should have pursued a more traditional and stabilizing path? All the questions flooded me with doubt in my ability to make the best decision in this next season of life. So when my senior year arrived, I applied to all different kinds of jobs and graduate schools as I was trying to navigate what I was going to do. After months of applying, interviewing, and discerning, I ended up torn between two final options. I could either work as an admission counselor at my undergrad institution or travel as a consultant for my sorority.

I was conflicted between these two options. I loved my university more than any other place in the world. To me, Texas Christian University is the Disney World of universities. It energized me to imagine myself being in a position where I was helping other high schoolers achieve their dreams of becoming a Horned Frog. I loved to travel, and I loved to talk to people, so that was a given in both jobs. Two things struck me about the admission opportunity, though. One, I am empathetic and inclusive, meaning that I would feel heartbroken every time I had to deliver a rejection to a hopeful high schooler. And two, this job opportunity may have meant that I wasn't going to leave Texas for a long time. I had been in Texas my whole life already, and I didn't know what else was out there. Don't get me wrong, like most Texans, I LOVE Texas, but there was this yearning inside me to see the rest of the country and what it could offer me. I wasn't sure if I was ready to "settle down."

When I considered the job as a sorority consultant, I became nervous and excited at the same time. The pay was significantly lower than the job in admission, and it was barely going to be enough to pay rent. I would have to ask my parents for help financially, and I wasn't sure if I wanted to continue to depend on them right after college. It was also only a one-year to two-year contracted job, so I would have to move onto something else pretty soon again. Did I really want to have to go through all this in another year or two? Despite these concerns, I couldn't shake how excited I was about the opportunity to travel and meet so many new people, helping them grow and develop.

I eventually decided to work as the consultant for my sorority because, in my gut, I knew that taking the admission job was more about security and comfort than about what energized me most. The sorority job was riskier, but I knew an opportunity to travel like this wouldn't come around again in this particular way. In that season of life, traveling, meeting different people, and developing my more business-y strengths were more important to me. Looking back now, I am so thankful I made that decision and trusted myself.

When we are in liminal seasons, on the brink of transition, trying to determine our next best step, it can feel overwhelming when we have to finally choose. Sometimes you want the answer to magically drop down from the sky and tell you what's next and what you should do. Having a choice is a blessing and a curse in that way. **It can be intimidating to take ownership of these big decisions, but you won't mess it up as long as you honor what you believe is best for you.** We can learn how to trust and listen to our authentic selves.

Intuition

Have you ever experienced that "gut feeling?" That deep knowing in your soul that something is right or wrong? That is your intuition. We all have it; just some of us recognize it better than others. We tend to quickly dismiss our intuition as a legitimate source of help when making decisions, but it has a lot to offer. Intuition is more than just a fleeting sensation we have in a moment. According to the science behind intuition, it is not based solely on feeling or emotion. Rather, it is logic that the brain has stored up through schemas based on your past experiences.[36] Meaning, the brain stores what you've learned through past happenings, and when you feel your gut talking to you, that's your body recalling your past to alert you for your future.

When I was making my job decision in college, I could not shake the gut feeling that I would live with regret for not taking the consulting job. All logic said to choose the admission counselor job because it provided more security. Still, something within me could not imagine saying no to the consultant opportunity. It's like my soul was speaking to me, saying, "Just for now…don't listen to your head, don't focus on how this looks on paper, rather how does it feel in your heart?" As they say, I went with my gut and am so thankful I did. Of course, it is crucial to consider the logistics involved with decision-making, especially with something like a job regarding salary or location. But after I've thought all my reasons through and am still just sitting on the decision, I know it's time to turn inward.

More often than not, I'm avoiding the commitment to a decision because I'm afraid, not because I don't know what I want. It is helpful to cultivate a practice of listening to our gut and trusting our intuition to gain the confidence and assurance we need to make our best decisions.

In her article on intuition, Renee Goyeneche gives us three ways to cultivate better recognition for what our intuition is trying to tell us. We can pay attention to physical cues, which might mean listening to the neurotransmitters in our bodies that make us feel a certain way. This means literally paying attention to that "gut" feeling I described earlier. We can write down the flashes of intuition that might surface in the form of "aha" moments, which will help us with decision-making later on. We can look back on all those insightful moments to inform us of what decision is best for us. And finally, we must take time to listen to our intuition, which is the most effective and simultaneously the most challenging practice for most of us.[37]

I am what my therapist calls a Highly Sensitive Person, meaning that I love big lights and sounds and all the things to stimulate my senses. This is probably why I love teaching indoor cycling classes so much – the music and lights and the bigness of it all helps me get lost in the moment. Therefore, you might imagine that my worst enemy is silence, and you would be right.

Total silence freaks me out. I'm that gal who needs a little bit of background noise to focus entirely. If it's too quiet, I get more distracted. You know that student who opens their bag of chips in the quiet section of the library, and everyone stares at them for disrupting the silence? I don't mind. Enjoy your Baked Lays! If it ushers in some noise, I'm grateful.

Knowing I am not super comfortable with quiet, I surprised myself when I enrolled in a class that required small group sessions with an hour of silence each week. I was a little nervous and very skeptical. The course was called Spirituality and Discernment. In this class, we learned decision-making practices that involved looking within ourselves for answers. Part of this class included engaging in a Quaker practice called a Clearness Committee once a week. At these meetings, we would help the focus person of the week think through and make a decision. It was fifty minutes of silence interspersed with questions. You read correctly. I didn't say fifty minutes of questions, but fifty minutes of silence with some questions sprinkled in. My overly stimulated self's worst nightmare. But that's what we did. We sat in silence and let the Spirit move. And it was amazing.

The first few sessions, I was squirmish, unsure, and skeptical. The silence made me restless, and I wanted to ask all the questions. The self-awareness I gained about what a chatter I am, how much I love to talk, and how little I actually listen was incredibly humbling. My classmates had excellent questions to offer that I would never have let surface if I had taken over. There were so many moments when I wanted to speak and ask a question, but instead, I would refrain. When I did this, someone else would ask the exact same question I was simmering on. It was beautiful to witness the Universe moving in this way amongst a group of acquaintances. It was in the silence that both my classmates and I could hear God move the most. In the silence, we listened to our own intuitions speaking.

To discover our most authentic selves and, therefore, live into our vocation, we first have to get quiet enough to hear our inner voice. In her book *Untamed*, Glennon Doyle describes this deep, sure recognition of our authentic, inner voice as the Knowing. She says it feels like it is filling her body with warm liquid gold as she sinks deeper to discover it.[38] When we let ourselves get quiet enough to hear our innermost voices and longings, it leaves us feeling empowered and convicted to honor them. The hardest part is that once we have met our inner voice, we can't move forward and no longer honor it without a whole mess of emotions. **Once you know what your authentic self needs to be free, every choice you make that does not honor it will keep you trapped.** You will not be able to live into your authentic vocation if you do not listen to your gut. Doyle continues,

> I have learned that if I want to rise, I have to sink first. I have to search for and depend upon the voice of inner wisdom instead of voices of outer approval.

This saves me from living someone else's life. It also saves me a hell of a lot of time and energy. I just do the next thing the Knowing guides me toward, one thing at a time.[39]

We must quiet the noise to hear ourselves. As Doyle writes, this prevents us from being persuaded by everyone but ourselves. And this journey is all about getting to know you.

One practice that helps people listen to their intuition is meditation. I know I mentioned this earlier when talking about our dreams, but it is such an essential tool in getting to know our true selves that we are going to dive deeper into it now. Because it is so loud in the outside world, we have to engage in a practice that allows us to quiet the noise to listen within. Stillness and quiet are vital in listening to our own selves, which is more challenging for some of us than others. Meditation might sound intimidating, really difficult, or just something you don't want to do, and that's normal. It is not easy and takes time and discipline to develop. But the benefits are extraordinary, and if you are worried about making the "right" decision, this is a practice I highly recommend.

A simple way to begin your meditation practice is to get in a quiet place, close the door, and maybe put your headphones on to quiet down any noise that might try to invade your space. Set a timer for five minutes. It doesn't sound like much, but trust me, it might feel like five years once you connect with your breath and begin to sink in. Then place your feet on the ground or sit crisscross applesauce (as I used to say), close your eyes, and breathe deeply.

You can breathe in for four counts, hold for seven, and exhale for eight. You could simply count your breaths. Or you could just breathe normally. The point is that all you are focused on is your breath. You calm your mind down enough to get beautifully still. And you listen to what comes up. Things will pop up in your mind that might be related to the decision or not, and you just acknowledge them and let them float on.

If it helps, intentionally bring the decision you are wrestling with to mind and notice how your body reacts. Does your breathing change? Your posture? Your stomach muscles? Notice these slight or significant changes as you consider your decision. Maybe you recall the two options you are weighing. Pretend like you are holding one in each hand. Does one feel weightier than another? How does it feel? Smell? Can you visualize yourself in these roles? What would you be wearing? Where is your office? How do these decisions make you feel?

Then, when you are ready, simply bring your attention to your breath, slowly flutter your eyes open, and return to the present moment. I fully believe that going internal with your decision will bring up helpful factors that you may not explore otherwise. Visualization and meditation are incredible tools for decision-making, so don't shy away. Remember, God can move in a multitude of ways. Start small. Start with short sessions. And, most importantly, start with intention. That is the most critical part of all of this. If this is not your genuine desire, if you don't really want to hear the hard truth that lies within you, then you won't. But, if you remain open, then get ready to see what the Spirit has in store for you. Self-discovery can be equally empowering as it is scary.

Pros / Cons

For those who might be looking for another tangible way to help make their decision, we turn to a trusty pro-con list. I made many pro-con lists when deciding what job to take after graduating. The mess of my lists accurately reflected my messy inside turmoil over what job to take. These weren't fancy lists, either. For example, the pro-con list on my computer was literally titled, "Ugh, my FUTURE." I can be a tad dramatic at times. The truth is, you can make pro-con lists until you are blue in the face. You can think of reasons for and reasons against your decisions for days on end. Ultimately, when it comes to pro-con lists, it is most helpful and efficient to consider the weight of your reasons more than the length of your lists.

It is essential to reflect on your lists and consider the weightiest or most important things to you. Too often, we gravitate toward whatever options on our lists have the most pros or the least cons. Let's consider an example. You are torn between two jobs – one that would require you to move to a new state or one in your hometown. The job in the new state has a list of pros and benefits a mile long, but only one con. The con is that it would take you away from your family. Now, if we just looked at the length of the lists, we would assume that taking the job in the new state is the best decision. But, for you, being near your family is one of your highest priorities and caring for your family is one of your top values. Choosing the new job based on the length of the list alone would be unwise, since the one con of moving away holds more weight than all the others combined. See how this works? You must make the best decision for YOU based on what you value and prioritize.

Every individual is different in what they value, so you must take time to get to know yourself before making any big decisions. A lot will come into play here, and a con for you might not be a con for someone else. Own what you need, and don't be afraid to be honest with yourself about that in this process. Remember the weight over the length.

Other People

The last place I look for validation is myself. If I am in the middle of making a big decision, heck, even a small one, I will consult at least five others before deciding. If you ask me where I want to go for dinner, I'll respond, "Oh, I don't know! Wherever you want to go is fine with me!" And then we'll go somewhere I don't even like, but I won't speak up. Yup, I'm THAT friend. Still working through my people-pleasing tendencies, but I'm learning.

We cannot allow the opinions or even helpful advice of others to make our decisions for us. Especially not regarding big, life-altering decisions like how you live out your vocation. Like I've mentioned, your values are your values, and your priorities are your priorities.

No one else is living your unique life with your unique giftings. Even if you have an identical twin, they cannot offer what you specifically bring to this world.

Now, I'm not saying that looking to others for wisdom, guidance, and advice is bad because others are a gift in our lives and a source of inspiration that we should consult. I just want to encourage you to look inward first. Before you look to others, dig a little deeper, do some internal work, and quiet the noise. Make the pro-con list. Listen to your intuition. Pray. Sleep on it. Maybe even a dream speaks to you? Just give yourself space to marinate on the decision before you welcome another voice.

When you do decide it is time to consult others, choose wisely. If you talk to too many people about this decision, you might become confused by all the varying opinions. The loud volume of everyone else will drown out your internal voice. There is no exact science here, but I suggest you choose three people to confide in regarding the big decisions. I would talk to a mentor who provides you wisdom, a best friend who wants what is genuinely best for you, and someone in the industry who has experience in what you are considering. And that's it! Of course, you might need to consult with your family, as well, but, outside of those three individuals, you are good to go. When we start asking too many people about what we should do, we seek validation more than advice. It's tempting to want to outsource the hard work of decision-making, but it will be ultimately up to you at some point. **No one else can make this decision for you.**

When I was deciding whether to take the consulting job or not, I called so many people who had considered the job opportunity before but had not taken it. Hearing them talk about how they regretted not doing it influenced me to consider the uniqueness of the opportunity at hand. I am grateful for the perspectives they shared with me, yet even among the regretters, some said I should do it, and others said I shouldn't. I once again realized that this process had to be rooted in honoring myself. They could tell me their experiences, but they couldn't tell me what to do.

Also, here's the thing. All the books and podcasts you can consult on how to make decisions will discuss what we are chatting about here. They might be very helpful, but they still cannot make this decision for you. I remember feeling so frustrated after listening to a podcast one time on decision-making because once it was over, I was thinking, "Well, God…THAT didn't make things any clearer!!" Because, news flash, the host didn't know my situation, values, or what was important to me! All they could do was remind me of the truth I already knew – that God would provide and be faithful in any decision I did make. Now THAT is some truth. Trust that you have what you need.

No Wrong Decision

You are not going to make a wrong decision. You will not mess this up. Even if you said no to all your current options, you wouldn't be making a "bad" decision. It is not a failure even if you pick the option that ends up being "wrong" for you and you hate your first job or break up with your partner. **We fail only if we choose not to learn from our experiences.** With that in mind, we can decide with confidence because every opportunity is one where we can learn and grow.

There is no wrong decision because I believe that God will use every single thing that happens in your life with purpose. Hear me closely. This is not me trying to say that everything that happens in your life is for "good" necessarily because some things in life just suck. Still, I do believe there is purpose in every circumstance, decision, and experience. Every decision reveals something about ourselves. Often, the decision-making process isn't even about what the decision is, but rather what you learn about yourself and the Universe through the process. Author Emily Freeman says it this way, "I'm learning that the decision is rarely the point. The point is becoming more fully ourselves in the presence of God, connecting with God and with each other, and living our lives as though we believe God is good and beautiful."[40] As you continue making decisions, you will learn more about yourself and how to honor your truest self through the choices you make. There is no right or wrong, only growth.

I recently asked one of my friends what she was most proud of herself for, and she responded, "Quitting my job." She found her authentic self in the decision-making process and made a choice based on what she had learned she needed. Remember, this self-discovery journey is about honoring you, however that manifests in this season. That's the only thing you have to worry about. Know yourself. Honor yourself. Decide. Trust. Make decisions rooted in love, not fear.

Start Here:

1. Make a pro-con list for your decision, marinating on the weight of the reasons rather than the length of the lists.
2. Hold a five-minute meditation session. Bring your decision to mind in your session and notice how you feel.
3. Reach out to a mentor, a best friend, and a colleague to gain their insight on your decision.
4. If you feel paralyzed to make the decision, ask yourself if it is because you genuinely don't know what to do, or because you are afraid of the outcome. If it's rooted in fear, dig into that a bit more. Take time to reflect and remind yourself of your unshakeable truths.
5. Do you trust yourself to make the right decision for you? Why or why not?

8

Confidence

QUEER EYE IS MY ALL-TIME favorite show. I will never forget watching the Fab 5 for the first time in Season One in Georgia. I was blown away by the power of their presence and passion. On the show, these five fierce experts on different areas of life help another person, called the hero, heal and transform into a more confident, proud, and loving version of themselves. I cry almost every episode because watching these people fall in love with themselves is one of the most powerful metamorphoses to witness. Through the work they do, the Fab 5 infuses confidence back into these heroes as they emerge from a week of work into prouder people.

Building confidence is key to owning any transitional experience. Discovering new things about ourselves can be scary as we are not always sure how things might turn out. Our confidence can be shaken in times of uncertainty, particularly when we are not even sure of what we control anymore. When making a new decision, there is much room for self-doubt to take root and make itself comfortable in our minds. But I want you to remember this: **your confidence rests in who you are, not what you do.** You can make any decision or walk into any room with the confidence of a boss, even if you are actually shaking in your boots, when you know you are honoring who you are. Confidence does not solely come by achieving or mastering external accomplishments. Confidence can be cultivated internally, within you, by honoring your authentic self and what you know you need. Let's dig into how.

Confidence-Boosting Toolkit

When you live in alignment with your authentic self, you will find confidence in liminal seasons of life. You know the power, potential, gifts, and skills you have to offer the world. You have taken the time to befriend your intuition. You have made your decision. Now we focus on rebuilding our confidence in ourselves to own it.

There are many different techniques or tips one can use to build their confidence in themselves. Briefly revisiting the idea of personal power, cultivating confidence in yourself is something personal to you that no one else can take from you. Yes, as humans, we will ultimately allow others to shake our confidence, but that is why it is so important for you to be equipped with a confidence-boosting toolkit. You will be able to refer to your toolkit whenever you need a reminder of the badass you are. You get to decide what goes in your toolkit. I will make some suggestions here for what might be helpful, but ultimately you choose what works best for you. Take some time and really develop these tools to have them as resources to rely on when your confidence is shaken or lagging. When someone wants to make us doubt ourselves, we can reach inward, knowing we have the personal power to stay in control of our self-belief.

So within this toolkit, we will have an array of options for you to choose from. This could range from pumping yourself up with affirmations, singing your favorite song, or wearing your favorite heels in your bedroom. This stuff might seem cheesy or overrated to you, but trust me, it works! It is essential to develop your own confidence-boosting toolkit because you have to believe in yourself first at the end of the day. You can't wait until others believe in you to believe in yourself and your dreams. You have to walk into this new season and opportunity with fierce confidence, believing you can do it, so others do too.

Your confidence-boosting toolkit will equip you for what you need to cheer yourself on in your new, challenging, and somewhat scary endeavor. These are going to be the rituals and resources you can turn to when you begin doubting your potential. And the best part? This toolkit will be completely self-oriented, meaning none of these resources or rituals will depend on anyone else validating you or believing in you. You can do this, and having these tools handy when doubt begins knocking will help empower you to shut that dang door, hold your head high, and move forward. Here are some of my favorite resources and rituals to have in my confidence-boosting toolkit. Of course, I invite you to add in your own, but here are a few of my recommendations to get started:

Affirmations

I'm sure you have heard of positive affirmations before, and I know they can feel silly sometimes, but there is legitimate psychological research behind their power. Psychologists call this the self-affirmation theory, which supports that we can maintain our sense of self-integrity by telling ourselves what we believe in positive ways.[41] Essentially, this means that we can preserve our strong sense of self-worth by stating what we want to think about ourselves positively. Consider this. When someone else tries to put you down or shake your confidence, your body and mind perceive that as a threat to you. But, by engaging in practices such as positive affirmations, we become more fortified against those threats as we consistently build our sense of self rooted in our beliefs and values.

Affirmations have to be personal to be effective. They can't just be these broad, generic statements about success or confidence. Instead, they need to be in alignment with what you personally value.[42] Psychologist Catherine Moore says it this way, "There is little point in repeating something arbitrary to yourself if it doesn't gel with your own sense of what you believe to be good, moral, and worthwhile. To have any kind of impact on your self-esteem, your self-affirmations should be positively focused and targeted at actions you can take to reinforce your sense of self-identity."[43] When developing your self-affirmations, consider your values and write them into your statements. Again, suppose the affirmation is about general success or happiness but does not align with what you actually value. In that case, it will not have the intended impact that it could.

There are a few different ways we can practice our self-affirmations. I suggest writing them down in a journal, on your phone, or even on your mirror in your bathroom. Saying your affirmations to yourself in your mirror may seem trivial at first, but it is a solid method for making them more powerful and effective.[44] I also like writing mine on sticky notes and sticking them around my desk space or in my car so that I am reminded of them throughout my day. Research recommends practicing your affirmations three to five times a day to reinforce the beliefs but anywhere is a good place to begin.[45] Some examples to get you started are:

I celebrate my best self today.

I embrace this day as a chance to develop and grow.

I maintain a positive attitude today, despite any hurdles that come my way. I have what it takes to succeed.

I am patient with myself and accept that positive change takes time. My best self is emerging every day.

I let go of my need to impress other people. There is nothing that I need to prove. I accept myself just as I am.

Encouragement Folder

We will all have those days when something or someone shakes our confidence. When this happens, it can be helpful to have reminders of the impact we have already made in the world to remind us of how capable we are. I have a photo album on my phone titled "Encouragement," and it is filled with screenshots of encouraging messages I have received from people over the years about my work or myself. When I doubt if I can do something or am good at what I do, I go back to that folder and read a few words of encouragement I've received, affirming that what I do and what I offer the world makes a difference. We won't receive affirmation from others daily about what we are doing, especially if the work we're going through is very behind-the-scenes. The encouragement folder is one effective way to remind yourself of the difference you make and reinforce your motivation to keep going!

Daily & Weekly Successes / Point of Pride

Self-reflection is a beautiful way to affirm ourselves and help us stay on the path of growth. We have to find ways to be proud of ourselves and celebrate our small wins, especially with long-term goals. Otherwise, we will be waiting quite some time to feel accomplished. One of my favorite questions to ask others is, "What are you proud of yourself for?" because the answers can range so greatly. When I began using this prompt for reflection in my own life, it permitted me to be proud of anything that day! It could be a step toward a goal I hit, something outside of my comfort zone, a hard conversation, doing something I'd been avoiding, or anything else. We can always search for ways to make ourselves proud without needing recognition from others. Cultivating a sense of pride helps us celebrate the small wins and remain grateful for our growth.

You can frame this exercise in two ways. You can use it as a prompt at the beginning of your day or week to consider what you could do to make you feel proud. Or you can use it as a tool for self-reflection at the end of the day or week to look back and reflect on what you did that made you proud. Having a strong sense of pride in ourselves and what we aim for is significantly helpful in rebuilding our confidence.

When I have a lot of hurdles in my way, I also like to take five minutes and brain dump a success list. These are all the things I've done that I define as success (this is big here!) Only you have the power to determine what success is for you, so don't shy away from writing down something "small" just because it may not look like success by society's standards. Remember, what is most important along this journey is living in alignment with what matters to YOU, so you get to have the final say in what makes you proud. These practices of reflecting on our successes will help boost our self-esteem as we continue to fortify and solidify our worthiness.

Music

I am a big believer in the power of a good playlist. Music has the potential to shift our mood and energy into whatever direction we want it to go. Sometimes, you want to put on music to lean into some kind of way you're feeling. While there is purpose in that, the music I'm referring to today is the playlist and music you need to pump yourself UP. The music you need to boost your confidence and shift your energy from one of doubt and discouragement to one of fired up ready to rock encouragement! I'm talking about Lizzo's "Good as Hell" or literally anything by Lady Gaga. Think of it this way. The purpose of this music is similar to the walk-up songs every player gets in baseball as they're approaching the home plate when it's their turn to bat. This is your "walk-up" music to life.

Maybe you're getting nervous about an interview for a new opportunity. Maybe you're about to have a challenging conversation with someone about a change you're making. Maybe you just woke up today and aren't feeling confident in yourself (we ALL have those days!) Cue your confidence-boosting playlist. If you don't know where to start, Spotify and Apple Music have playlists already created with this intention in mind. You can always begin with inspiration from others!

Remember, you have the power to shift your energy if that is what you want. As I once heard Oprah say, you are responsible for the energy you bring to your space. So if you need to shift your energy or pump yourself up and augment your mood, have a playlist or a favorite album or artist cued up and ready to go.

Power Posing

Power posing is another way to build up your confidence, particularly before a big event or something you've never done before. This is when you engage in specific postures that help expand your body language and take up space. In her book, *Presence,* Dr. Amy Cuddy writes, "Expanding your body language - through posture, movement, and speech - makes you feel more confident and powerful, less anxious and self-absorbed, and generally more positive."[46] **Physiologically, we must tell our brains and our hearts that we have permission to take up space, and we deserve to be in the rooms we are in.** So get expansive! Stand up tall, lift your chin, put your hands on your hips, or take a big stretch. The bigger the better! Want to make a confidence-boosting sandwich? Stand in front of a mirror in a power pose and recite your affirmations to yourself. That's a triple threat right there.

You Do You

So, to get your confidence-boosting toolkit started, you have your power poses, points of pride, music, encouragement folder, and self-affirmations. Don't let this overwhelm you, though. You don't have to wake up tomorrow and implement all these suggestions. Over time they can build up to become the resources you might reach for at any given moment of confidence-shaking. Maybe you start with the one that excited you the most and give it a try! Or maybe you have your own techniques you already love to use, and you just sprinkle some of these suggestions in. This is all about finding what works best for you, so whatever that is, you do you. These tactics aren't only helpful in fighting the threats to your confidence from others, but also from the sneaky impostor that can come from within.

Start Here:

1. Which suggestion excited you the most? How might you implement it into your routine this week?
2. Write down three positive affirmations and put them somewhere you will be reminded of them daily. Remember to align them with your personal values!
3. Begin creating a confidence-boosting playlist. Pick five songs that make you feel fierce and confident and drop them in.
4. Pop open that journal and brain dump a success list of all you accomplished last week. Again, these don't only have to be "big" things – the daily successes we might look past matter too!
5. How else do you boost your confidence internally? Is there anything else you already do that helps you to feel good about yourself? Add them to your toolkit!

9

IMPOSTOR SYNDROME

I ABSOLUTELY LOVE INDOOR CYCLING classes. I mean, from the first time I clipped onto a bike and felt the music surrounding me, I was hooked. Well, maybe not from the very first class because, to be honest, I cried during that class because I was so frustrated with the pedals. But after that…obsessed. These classes have become a sacred space of healing throughout my life. When I first began attending indoor cycling classes, I was struggling with my mental health, particularly my belief in myself big time. Every time I went to class, I completely released any stress or anxiety I felt by getting lost in the music and movement. What helped me rebuild my confidence significantly, though, was the instructor. Hearing someone believe in me, even if they didn't know me, meant the world to me during that season of life. I needed to hear someone else tell me that I could do this. And by going consistently, my confidence in myself was reshaped and sustained. So when I heard that my studio was holding auditions to become an instructor, I signed up immediately. I figured that since I loved it so much, I might as well give it a try. Fast forward six months later, after weeks and weeks of training and a few logistical delays, and I was ready to teach my first class. I was nervous as hell but anxiously filled with excitement for this new chapter in my life.

The first class I taught was a sub for someone else. I didn't think twice about it at first, but then all these fears and doubts began to creep into my mind. I began to worry that they wouldn't like me as much as the other instructor or that they would be disappointed they had to ride with the new girl instead of their more experienced instructor. The class happened, I overthought it the entire time, and then I left feeling super weird. To be clear, the class was good! I didn't mess up or anything, but I began to sob as soon as I got to my car.

I felt overwhelmed, insecure, and like I had been exposed. Me? A fitness instructor? FRAUD! This isn't who you are, Meredith! You've never done this before. Who are you to think you can lead and step into this arena?

Wow. The little voices in our heads sure can get loud when we start to doubt. And the most vulnerable place for doubt to creep in is when we start something new. When we do something that people don't know us for…yet. Something that we don't feel entirely prepared for. Well, if anyone else hasn't told you, I'll bust the myth for us all right now: **no one begins something new as an expert**. We all wrestle with doubt and insecurity when being a beginner.

In this scenario, I was stuck in a severe case of impostor syndrome. Impostor syndrome is the belief that you are not equipped to do the thing you are doing, and therefore, you feel like a fraud and that people will "find out" and expose you as such. It usually arises when we are beginning something new. Google Dictionary defines impostor syndrome as "the persistent inability to believe that one's success is deserved or has been legitimately achieved as a result of one's own efforts or skills." Impostor syndrome is not based on fact but belief.

Because here's the thing: in my scenario, I had spent the last six months training one-on-one with one of the best indoor cycling instructors in the country. I had ridden almost every day, taking diligent notes to reflect and improve after every class. And I was beyond ready for this first class. It wasn't a question of whether my effort and skill were enough for the task, but if I believed I deserved it. Did I believe in myself? Did I believe I was worthy of the result of my hard work? Did I deserve to pursue this dream I had spent so much time on?

Answer: YES, and the same goes for you. In a season of total unknown, it is so easy to doubt our own skills and efforts that can open new doors for us. And, when our lives have been shaken up, sometimes we have to be the ones who open new doors when others close. If we don't want to be a victim to our circumstances and if we're going to be the authors of our own lives, then we have to take ownership of what we can offer the world. And yes, this is scary, especially when it is something you've never done before, but let me share from the little experience I have that it is always worth it.

This is the first book I've ever written, so I am feeling some significant impostor syndrome as I am typing these words right now. But I believe I have a skill and a passion that can help others, so I choose to believe in myself despite the doubt that can creep in. When people ask me what I am doing, I try to boldly own and share that I am an aspiring author writing my first book. As I hear the words coming out of my mouth, I want to retract them almost immediately for fear of how others will respond, but you know what has been the most surprising? Everyone I've shared with has been cheering me on. And some of them don't even know if I can write well or not! Some of them barely know me, but there is something about someone going after their dream that makes others want to root for them. I know the world can be really scary and sucky sometimes, but I'm learning that people are more eager and willing to cheer you on in your new endeavors than you might think. Is it wild to say that others might actually want you to succeed? Don't be afraid to own what you are going after.

Impostor syndrome is one major way to self-sabotage our progress toward our goals. We get in our heads and assume that others are judging us for going after our dreams or being innovative with the skills we've developed. Or, at least I do. I feel so exposed when I do something that I've worked toward for the first time. And it IS scary, don't question that. But this is where those confidence-building tools will help sustain you. This is where your clear definition and commitment to your values and dreams carry you through. This is where you access your intuition that tells you that these doubts are just lies and you are worthy of pursuing your goal. Every human is susceptible to impostor syndrome, and most people will encounter it at some point in their lives. It has been around for a long time, even if we didn't have a formal name for it.

History of Impostor Syndrome

Dr. Pauline Rose Clance and Suzanne Imes coined the term impostor syndrome as they began to investigate why their counseling clients were experiencing the crippling doubt and belief that they were frauds in what they were doing. From this research, Dr. Clance created a measuring scale to determine if someone suffered from impostor syndrome. In 1978, they published their first academic paper on the topic. At the beginning of the discovery of impostor syndrome, Dr. Clance believed it only affected women, for she only heard women describe these symptoms to her. She believed the condition was unique only to high-achieving women "since success for women is contraindicated by societal expectations and their own internalized self-evaluations, it is not surprising that women in our sample need to find an explanation for their accomplishments other than their own intelligence."[47] In short, not only did women not believe in themselves, but society also put an expectation on them that their intelligence was never enough. There had to be another reason why a woman could be successful – luck, a connection, or otherwise – not because she earned it.

Soon enough, via an analysis of anonymous surveys, Dr. Clance discovered that impostor syndrome affected both women and men equally. It appeared that women suffered significantly more from impostor syndrome because they talked about it more than men. When in reality, both men and women suffer from impostor syndrome. It is more socially acceptable for women to admit they struggle with impostor syndrome and feelings of self-doubt, while men cannot openly share without often risking ridicule from their peers. According to the status quo, men are not allowed to be vulnerable or sensitive. Dr. Cuddy shares that "although men experience impostorism to the same extent women do, they may be even more burdened by it because they can't admit it. They carry it around quietly, secretly, painfully."[48] Men might suffer more intensely from impostor syndrome because the shame for feeling like a fraud keeps them from sharing their struggles with anyone else. It is a horrible feeling to think you have to hide who you are and what you're going through from everyone else. Pretty much everyone experiences impostor syndrome at some point in their lives. Perhaps we can all feel more empowered to be vulnerable and permit others to do the same by understanding it more.

It is not just the difference between men and women that needs to be considered regarding impostor syndrome. Minorities, particularly people of color, are significantly affected by impostorism. According to research by Dr. Kevin Cokley, a professor of educational psychology and African diaspora studies at the University of Texas at Austin, impostor syndrome can intensify discrimination some minority groups already experience, only adding to their stress.[49] It is essential to recognize that women and people of color are more vulnerable to impostor syndrome on top of the discrimination they already might experience in the workplace and beyond. No matter what demographic you identify with, everyone can experience impostor syndrome, and the root causes are difficult to pin down. There are simply too many reasons why one might suffer from it.

I appreciate what Dr. Clance had to say to Dr. Cuddy about how she came up with the name impostor syndrome, for I believe it removes the shame we might feel from it. She said, "If I could do it all over again, I would call it the impostor experience, because it's not a syndrome or a complex or a mental illness. It's something almost everyone experiences."[50] If there is one thing you take away from this chapter, it's that **you are not alone in your experience of impostor syndrome**. It's okay to own your doubts or fears, for the impostor in you will only continue to gain power the more you hide it away. You are not alone in this.

Transition = Impostor Opportunity

We are especially vulnerable to impostor syndrome when stepping into something new or claiming a new identity, which a lot of us experience when navigating liminal seasons. It is vital to acknowledge your honest emotions around this new thing and not suppress them. Starting something new can be very scary to embrace, especially if you wrestle with the fear of how others will respond. After you acknowledge your emotions, I want you to challenge them with the truth – that you CAN do this, and you ARE here because you have worked hard and deserve it. Feeling nervous is normal. If we aren't a little scared stepping into our dreams, that might indicate that they aren't big enough. We have to believe that God honors our heartfelt goals and wants them for us, too! The Message version of Ephesians 3:20-21 says it this way, "God can do anything, you know – far more than you could ever imagine or guess or request in your wildest dreams! He does it not by pushing us around but by working within us, his Spirit deeply and gently within us."

God wants you to dream bigger. I do not believe God created you with all your unique talents and skills that you can offer this world to have them squashed by fear and disbelief. Do you think you're dreaming big? God imagines more for your life. It's up to us to affirm that we are worthy of those good and big dreams of ours. And I love the second line of this verse – that God will do this work because the Spirit is already profoundly and gently working in us. Of course, we need to look outside of ourselves for help and resources, but we also need to remember to look within and trust that God has equipped us with everything we need to thrive. The Universe is always at work, even when our world, careers, or goals can feel stagnant.

Defeating Our Inner Impostor Strategies

If there is one thing for certain, it is that impostor syndrome will come in and affect your life at some point, especially if you are transitioning into something new. So how can we combat impostor syndrome when it comes? In her article, "4 Ways to Combat Impostor Syndrome," Lisa Rogoff suggests four different tips to help us fight our inner impostor, commentaries are mine.[51]

1. *Get to know your impostor and take back control* – Rogoff suggests giving your inner impostor a name, which I absolutely loved, so I named mine Sheila. I think of Sheila as similar to anxiety. She might live with me in the room, but I don't have to give her control or a voice. I can acknowledge that Sheila is there, but I don't have to give her power or space to speak. Sheila, you might be here, but it is MY turn to talk.

2. *Find comfort in others* – One thing research shows is that we do not suffer from impostor syndrome alone. So many CEOs and leaders in major fields have felt like impostors at one time or another. As Tiny Fey once said, "Seriously, I've just realized that almost everyone is a fraud, so I try not to feel too bad about it." When we share our impostor with others, we immediately will feel less alone. And, if the person you share with cares about their work, they probably have also experienced this in some way. They will be able to resonate with your experience. Once you realize everyone thinks they're a fraud, you have permission to move forward, feeling a little less silly about yourself. No one knows what they're doing, especially when they're getting started. So just go!

3. *Use the facts to prove your impostor wrong* – When I really want to shut Sheila up, I'll start declaring my success list. For real, if my impostor is loud and is trying to tell me that I am a fraud and I cannot do this new thing, I will come back at her with my laundry list of what a badass I am. I'll declare and call to mind all the hard, new, challenging things I have accomplished in the past. I'll remember the other complicated, and scary seasons I overcame, believing that I have what it takes to do it again. What you have accomplished in your past is a FACT, not an opinion. Look back to your success list we brainstormed in the confidence chapter and speak it aloud.

4. *Let go of perfect and just do it* – This is hands-down my favorite suggestion. **If we wait until we're ready, we will never get started.** When the rubber meets the road, you have to put pen to paper, send in that application, or post that video. At

some point, you have to want your vocation or dream or whatever it is bad enough not to care how perfect it is or what others will think of what you do or put into the world. You have got to just do it! As I began to write this book, one of my favorite exercises I did was creep on authors that I admire and want to emulate in some way in my work. These are the people whose careers I look at that make me think to myself, "Wow, this is THE GOAL! I want to be like ____ someday." To remind me that this individual is also a human being who was a beginner at one point in time, I go on Amazon and find their first published book. I see how different it is from what my role model is writing now. And let me tell you, this exercise permits me to let go of perfect and know that wherever I am starting at is enough. Any action step moves me closer to my dream. I mean, your choice is to either do it or not at the end of the day. And you'll never be perfect, so you might as well go for it!

Hopefully, these four tools to combat your impostor syndrome will help you challenge and overcome your impostor when they start speaking loudly. You have done the work of self-discovery, and I refuse to let you self-sabotage your way out of living into the freest and truest you. Impostor syndrome is just a nasty bully of fear, but you've done this work, and you deserve to go after what you want. Rogoff ends her article by sharing,

> Even if you're doing the best work, if you're constantly putting yourself down publicly and not owning your success, others will believe what you believe. And even if you keep your impostor feelings to yourself, you'll still internalize your self-limiting and self-sabotaging feelings and undermine your decisions. Either way, the Impostor makes you live small.[52]

I don't want us to live small and fall under the false belief that we are alone in experiencing impostor syndrome. Don't give your inner doubter power. If and when this comes up for you, don't be alarmed. Remember, we all experience impostor syndrome at some point. At least now, we have some tools to combat it when it does arise. Trust that you are on the right path and that you can do this.

Start Here:

1. Have you experienced impostor syndrome before? What did it feel like?
2. Which one of the four tools feels most helpful for you? How can you incorporate it into your life right now?
3. What idea of perfection do you need to let go of to give yourself permission to get started?
4. Is there anyone in your life who has gone through a similar transition or experience of impostor syndrome you might be able to confide in?
5. Write down your factual success list to remind yourself that you can do this new and scary thing! Remind yourself, as Glennon Doyle says, that you can do hard things!

10

Own Your Worthiness

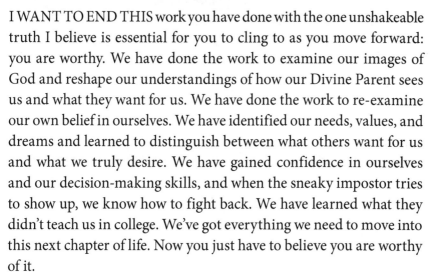

I WANT TO END THIS work you have done with the one unshakeable truth I believe is essential for you to cling to as you move forward: you are worthy. We have done the work to examine our images of God and reshape our understandings of how our Divine Parent sees us and what they want for us. We have done the work to re-examine our own belief in ourselves. We have identified our needs, values, and dreams and learned to distinguish between what others want for us and what we truly desire. We have gained confidence in ourselves and our decision-making skills, and when the sneaky impostor tries to show up, we know how to fight back. We have learned what they didn't teach us in college. We've got everything we need to move into this next chapter of life. Now you just have to believe you are worthy of it.

Life is a continuous cycle of change whether we realize it, like it, or not. The skills you have learned in this book will serve you well if you do the work. The foundational beliefs you examined and perhaps re-defined for yourself will be what ground you as change comes again. I hope this book can be a resource you can return to again and again when you need a reminder or a belief boost as you pursue your dreams.

No one else can do this work for you, though. It's up to you to use this time to grow and honor your authentic self. I believe that you bought this book because you want positive change from where you are at today. We must believe we are worthy of the work, or our motivation will fall short fast. One of my favorite authors, Jen Hatmaker, speaks of our worthiness in this way:

We fight for this in our own lives, so we can fight for it in everyone else's. We believe it for ourselves, so we can believe it for others. Grab hold of this truth, so you can look someone else in the eye and assure them they are worthy of good things, no matter what they've been told. Folks full of goodness are the ones we need. They are our best teachers, our kindest leaders, our healthiest parents, our most generous friends. **Do this work, so you can pour it back out on the people you love and live by, serve and cherish.** Fierce self-compassion pays its greatest dividends in the way we are able to love. Insist that you are worth the work, because the people you adore are worth your best.[53]

Hatmaker reminds us that not only is it essential to believe that you are worth this work, but it is critical to the betterment of people everywhere that you believe you are worthy. When you believe you are worthy of growth, love, and good things, then I might start to believe it for myself too. God doesn't value one of us more than another. We are ALL worthy of our dreams, but we all need help believing that sometimes. Be an example for others to find their worthiness.

As you grow through your time of transition, I hope you discover who you really are and build up the courage to pursue that most authentic version of yourself. When you do so, you will naturally produce a ripple effect that inspires others. Those who knew the "old" you won't be able to help notice the changes in you. They will celebrate and see the freest you emerging as a result of this work. They'll want to know how you became so happy and content amid such uncertainty, and you'll know it's because you took the time to discover and honor your authentic self.

As you continue your self-discovery journey, know that you are worthy of what you find. **Believe that you deserve to honor the truest you, and when you do so, you inspire others to believe the same for them.** You and you alone have done the self-discovery work, so don't be quick to give others the power over your life again. Remember, we stripped ourselves of that pressure chapters ago.

I hope you are proud of yourself for working through this book and beginning this self-discovery journey. It is the most worthwhile, life-long work I could encourage any of us to do. I'm here cheering you on, fully believing that you can discover and own your truest self as you emerge from this liminality. **You are on the threshold of something greater than you could have ever imagined for yourself.** Keep listening to yourself and keep dreaming big. You got this.

For Further Reading

Burnout by Emily & Amelia Nagoski

This is maybe one of my favorite books of all time, and I have gone back to read it multiple times. The introduction alone was immensely educational on the science behind burnout. Everyone experiences burnout, and many authors write about it. This book is set apart because the Nagoski sisters share the science behind burnout, why we experience it, and how we can step back into our power (particularly as women) to squash it. I loved their emphasis on connection and how they dive into how the patriarchy has led to women experiencing human giver syndrome. If you've wanted to unlock the secret to burnout, PLEASE read this book. It will make you feel less alone and like you have concrete steps to take. Understanding the science and the culture behind burnout also helps us feel less guilty. This book will help you look for signs of burnout, give you tools to complete your stress cycle, and empower you to rest, connect, and redefine success.

Dare to Lead by Brené Brown

Dare to Lead is one of Dr. Brown's most practical books and is a must-read particularly if you are in a leadership role. Her work on vulnerability in the context of leadership is groundbreaking and helps us learn how to lead with empathy. Specifically, her insight on feedback helps you learn how to best give and also receive feedback, which is essential to the growth and development of any individual and group. If you are curious to further understand values-based living and how they show up in our relationships with others, I would recommend this book.

Untamed by Glennon Doyle

If you have not read this book, stop what you're doing and add it to a shopping cart now! In *Untamed,* Doyle shares stories of her life that helped her see how she was conforming to who society told her she needed to be. This is the journey of Doyle discovering and living into her truest self. Safe to say, she definitely inspired me to write this book. The writing left me in tears multiple times, and all her work feels so relatable and accessible. She doesn't say it will be easy, but she encourages us all that, "We can do hard things." A must read.

Presence by Amy Cuddy

Presence is the research-backed confidence-boosting book I never knew I needed. Dr. Cuddy provides accessible skills to implement to help us get present in our bodies, stop worrying about what others think, and lean into how we perceive ourselves. She helps you trust yourself and cultivate the personal power you need to believe you can continue to do the hard things.

The Next Right Thing by Emily P. Freeman

This book is a faith-centered decision-making guide that helped me through so many tough choices. Through sharing stories, Freeman helps us understand how we can make the best decisions for ourselves by trusting God and focusing on the next right thing. The practices she shares to help you know what to decide, who to consult with, and how to know you are choosing the right thing for you are astronomically helpful. If you are in a decision-making bind, I highly recommend this book.

You Are a Badass by Jen Sincero

I devoured this book the first time I read it, and it is one of my most highly quoted texts I've read. *You Are a Badass* is a kick-in-the-pants wake-up call to how awesome you are. Sincero dives into why we are wired to see ourselves how we do and gives practical tools for getting out of those negative, self-defeating cycles. She also addresses healthy ways to think about money and building habits. Her voice is passionate, relatable, and fun throughout. Truly, this is a helpful book you'll enjoy reading.

Mindset by Carol S. Dweck

Dr. Dweck is the leading researcher on fixed and growth mindsets, and her book explains it all. This book is a bit denser as it dives into understanding and applying the psychology of success to areas of life like parenting, business, school, and relationships. If this idea struck you while reading this book, I highly recommend reading more of Dr. Dweck's work. It is very empowering to more deeply understand how a growth mindset can be attained and lead to success.

Author Biography

Meredith Trank cares deeply about helping people discover, believe in, and honor their truest selves. She is currently pursuing a Master of Divinity and a Master of Arts in Clinical Mental Health Counseling at Wake Forest University. A native Texan, she lives in North Carolina with her husband, Michael, and their adopted Puggle, Chunk. This is her debut book. To connect with her further, you can find her at @meredithktrank on Instagram or at meredithtrank.com.

References

[1] Julia Thomas, "Understanding How Liminal Space Is Different From Other Places | Betterhelp," accessed July 22, 2020, https://www.betterhelp.com/advice/general/understanding-how-liminal-space-is-different-from-other-places/.

[2] "Liminal Space," Center for Action and Contemplation, July 7, 2016, https://cac.org/liminal-space-2016-07-07/.

[3] Wilkie Au and Noreen Cannon Au, *The Discerning Heart* (New York: Paulist Press, 2006), 205-206.

[4] Howard Thurman, *Meditations of the Heart* (Boston: Beacon Press, 1953).

[5] "Understanding Liminal Space," Living Compass, accessed May 4, 2020, https://www.livingcompass.org/wwow/understanding-liminal-space.

[6] Elizabeth Liebert, *The Way of Discernment* (Louisville, KY: Westminster John Knox Press, 2008), 31.

[7] Brené Brown, *Braving the Wilderness* (New York: Random House, 2017), 40.

[8] Carol S. Dweck, *Mindset: The New Psychology of Success* (New York: Ballantine Books, 2016), 6.

[9] Ibid., 7.

[10] Ibid., 48.

[11] Amy Cuddy, *Presence: Bringing Your Boldest Self to Your Biggest Challenges* (New York: Little, Brown and Company, 2015), 113-115.

[12] "12 Tips For Building Self-Confidence and Self-Belief (+PDF Worksheets)," PositivePsychology.com, July 18, 2018, https://positivepsychology.com/self-confidence-self-belief/.

[13] "Social Comparison Theory | Psychology Today," accessed May 5, 2020, https://www.psychologytoday.com/us/basics/social-comparison-theory.

[14] "5 Ways to Stop 'Should'-Ing All Over Yourself," Jessi Kneeland, March 24, 2017, https://jessikneeland.com/stop-shoulding-yourself/.

[15] Kendra Cherry, "How Social Comparison Theory Influences Our Views on Ourselves," Verywell Mind, May 25, 2020, https://www.verywellmind.com/what-is-the-social-comparison-process-2795872.

[16] "The State of SleepHealth in America," SleepHealth, accessed April 1, 2021, https://www.sleephealth.org/sleep-health/the-state-of-sleephealth-in-america/.

[17] Emily Nagoski and Amelia Nagoski, *Burnout* (New York: Ballantine Books, 2020), 163.

[18] Molly Shea, "The 7 Types of Rest You Need to Actually Feel Recharged," Shine, accessed April 1, 2021, https://advice.theshineapp.com/articles/the-7-types-of-rest-you-need-to-actually-feel-recharged/.

[19] Nagoski, *Burnout*, 141.

[20] Ibid., 142.

[21] Saul Mcleod, "Maslow's Hierarchy of Needs," Simply Psychology, accessed May 12, 2020, https://www.simplypsychology.org/maslow.html.

[22] "5 Ways to Build Lasting Self-Esteem," *Ideas.Ted.Com* (blog), August 23, 2016, https://ideas.ted.com/5-ways-to-build-lasting-self-esteem/.

[23] Saundra Dalton-Smith, *Sacred Rest* (New York: Hachette Book Group, 2017), 127.

[24] Liz Russell, "3 Steps to Living in Alignment with Your Values," Medium, August 31, 2018, https://medium.com/@lizrusselll/know-your-values-know-you-d6c997cf5c5d.

[25] Brené Brown, *Dare to Lead* (New York: Random House, 2018), 186.

[26] Ibid., 187.

[27] Ibid.

[28] Anna Rowley, Shine Together: Anxiety Series, May 11, 2020.

[29] Carley Sime, "Please Get To Know Your Values," Forbes, accessed May 13, 2020, https://www.forbes.com/sites/carleysime/2019/01/25/please-get-to-know-your-values/.

[30] Linda Luke, "Living in Alignment with Your Values," Medium, August 24, 2017, https://medium.com/@lindaluke/living-in-alignment-with-your-values-9f8cd3f47ab1.

[31] Au, *The Discerning Heart*, 169.

[32] Jen Sincero, *You Are a Badass* (Philadelphia, PA: Running Pr Book Pub, 2013), 50.

[33] Parker Palmer, *Let Your Life Speak* (San Francisco, CA: Jossey-Bass, 2000), 10.

[34] Glennon Doyle, *Untamed* (New York: The Dial Press, 2020), 158.

[35] Ian Morgan Cron and Suzanne Stabile, *The Road Back to You* (Brentwood, TN: InterVarsity Press, 2016), 24.

[36] Renee Goyeneche, "How To Harness Intuition And Make Better Decisions," Forbes, accessed April 11, 2021, https://www.forbes.com/sites/womensmedia/2020/08/31/how-to-harness-intuition-and-make-better-decisions/.

[37] Ibid.

[38] Doyle, *Untamed*, 58.

[39] Ibid., 60.

[40] Emily P. Freeman, *The Next Right Thing* (Grand Rapids, MI: Revell, 2019), 157.

[41] Catherine Moore, "Positive Daily Affirmations: Is There Science Behind It?," PositivePsychology.com, March 4, 2019, https://positivepsychology.com/daily-affirmations/.

[42] Ibid.

[43] Ibid.

[44] Ibid.

[45] Barrie Davenport, "119 Positive Affirmations For Women (Get Your Daily Antidote to Negativity)," accessed April 13, 2021, https://liveboldandbloom.com/09/self-confidence/positive-affirmations-women.

[46] Cuddy, *Presence,* 216.

[47] Ibid., 92.

[48] Ibid., 94.

[49] Kristin Wong, "Dealing With Impostor Syndrome When You're Treated as an Impostor," *The New York Times*, June 12, 2018, sec. Smarter Living, https://www.nytimes.com/2018/06/12/smarter-living/dealing-with-impostor-syndrome-when-youre-treated-as-an-impostor.html.

[50] Cuddy, *Presence,* 95.

[51] Lisa Rogoff, "4 Ways to Combat Impostor Syndrome," Shine, accessed May 15, 2020, https://advice.shinetext.com/articles/4-ways-to-combat-impostor-syndrome/.

[52] Ibid.

[53] Jen Hatmaker, *Fierce Free and Full of Fire* (Nashville, TN: Nelson Books, 2020), 68.